# Contents

# Acknowledgments

Many people assisted in the work of putting this guide together. At the National Archives in Washington, D.C., Robert Ellis, Bill Davis, Rod Ross, and George Briscoe all assisted me in my search for records. Bill Davis and Rod Ross also read and commented on the chapters related to congressional records. At the National Archives at College Park, Maryland (Archives II), Gene Morris and Tab Lewis helped me locate records. Tab Lewis also read and commented on several chapters in Parts I and III. John VanDereedt, also of Archives II, read several chapters in Parts III and IV and made very helpful suggestions. Many archivists at the regional branches of the National Archives provided finding aids, answered questions, and photocopied records. These archivists include Jefferson Moak and Gail Farr of the National Archives at Philadelphia; Charles Miller of the National Archives at San Francisco; Randy Thompson of the National Archives at Riverside; Gregory Plunges of the National Archives at New York City; Greg Longacre of the National Archives at Chicago; Mary Evelyn Tomlin of the National Archives at Atlanta; and Joan Gearin of the National Archives at Boston. Nathaniel Wiltzen of the National Archives at Boston, and Diana Duff and Mark Corriston of the National Archives at Kansas City, offered helpful comments on Chapters 1 and 2.

Much of the research for this guide was conducted at libraries in Washington, D.C. The research librarians at the library of the Supreme Court of the United States—Catherine Romano, Jill Duffy, Joy Shoemaker, Linda Corbelli, Melissa Williams, and Sara Sonet—allowed me to use the stacks of the Court's library, which was helpful as I tracked down bibliographic records related to the judiciary. Elizabeth Endicott, at the library of the Administrative Office of the United States Courts, also assisted. Luis Acosta of the Law Library of Congress read and gave helpful comments on Chapter 4. Leona Faust of the U.S. Senate Library helped me locate materials related to Congress. Virginia Dunn of the Library of Virginia helped verify information for Appendix F.

Michael Courlander and Lisa Rich of the United States Sentencing Commission offered comments on the Sentencing Commission section of the guide.

Several of my colleagues at the Federal Judicial Center have offered indispensable assistance in the preparation of this guide. I. Scott Messinger began work on the guide several years ago, collecting much of the information necessary for its completion and providing me with drafts of several chapters. Steven Saltzgiver provided me with notes he had taken on records related to the executive branch administration of the federal courts and on courthouses. Robert Timothy Reagan offered me his knowledge of "unpublished" court opinions as well as of sealed and classified materials. Rozzie Bell tracked down dozens of books, articles, and finding aids. Jake Kobrick assisted in the compiling of Appendix F. Finally, I thank Bruce Ragsdale, director of the Federal Judicial History Office at the Federal Judicial Center, who envisioned this project and patiently guided it through to its completion.


Jonathan W. White

# Introduction to Historical Research in Federal Judicial History

This guide describes the records of the federal courts, as well as records of Congress and the executive branch, that are relevant to researching federal judicial history. Most federal records are held by the National Archives and Records Administration (NARA), either at NARA's main facilities in Washington, D.C., and College Park, Maryland, or at one of the National Archives' regional branches. Recent records may still be held by the government agency that created the records, or, pending their accession by the National Archives, at a Federal Records Center.

Records at the National Archives are organized into "record groups," with most government departments, offices, organizations, and agencies being assigned their own record group number. The records of the U.S. district courts, for example, are in Record Group (RG) 21, while the general records of the Department of the Treasury are in RG 56, and the records of the U.S. courts of appeals are in RG 276. Each chapter of this guide directs researchers to record groups related to various aspects of judicial history, as well as to materials that document the judiciary's relationship with the other two branches of the federal government.

In 1995, the National Archives published *The Guide to Federal Records in the National Archives of the United States*, which contains a brief description and inventory of each record group held by NARA; an online version (at http://www.archives.gov/research/guide-fed-records/) incorporates information about records received after 1995 and is updated regularly. Detailed descriptions of individual record groups also appear in the National Archives' online Archival Research Catalog (ARC), available at http://www.archives.gov/research/arc/index.html. Researchers can use ARC to find information about the content of each record group, as well as view selected documents that the National Archives has digitized and made available online.

The National Archives has published preliminary inventories for many of its record groups (see Appendix B). A preliminary inventory outlines the organizational structure of a record group and briefly describes the record group's contents. Most record groups have only one preliminary inventory; however, record groups that are held by more than one branch of the National Archives may have multiple inventories to describe the records maintained by individual regional branches. The records of the U.S. district courts in RG 21, for example, are organized by judicial district and are held at various regional branches in the NARA system. Accordingly, each regional branch has created a preliminary inventory or finding aid for the records of each judicial district whose records it holds.

Many of NARA's preliminary inventories were created more than 40 years ago and do not describe recently accessioned records. In some cases, record groups have been reorganized so that the preliminary inventories no longer accurately describe the arrangement of the records. In such cases, preliminary inventories are still a useful starting point for researchers to determine the basic scope and content of a record group, but researchers should confirm with an archivist that an inventory accurately describes the records the researchers plan to use.

The National Archives has created a "master location register" for each record group in the Washington, D.C., area, as well as for many of its holdings at the regional facilities. Master location registers are "in house" documents that the archivists use to locate records in the stacks. At many locations, however, researchers can use these registers to determine how many boxes or volumes are in a particular series within a record group, or to identify newly processed materials that are not described in *The Guide to Federal Records* or in a record group's preliminary inventory.

The National Archives has microfilmed many portions of its collections related to the federal judiciary, and a listing of microfilmed records is available at http://www.archives.gov/research/formats/microfilm.html. NARA's microfilmed records may be viewed at the main National Archives facilities in Washington, D.C., and College Park, Maryland, and at selected regional facilities; copies of microfilmed records may also be purchased.

The National Archives places prefatory information at the beginning of each reel of microfilm that it produces. For some reels this material is quite extensive, giving information about content down to the item level. Other reels only provide researchers with a brief explanation of the scope and type of records included in the collection. This prefatory material can help researchers determine which reels of microfilm to purchase, or how to locate particular records within NARA's microfilmed records. Researchers can download and print this prefatory material from any reel of NARA microfilm directly from the National Archives' website, http://www.archives.gov/order/.

The locations, hours of operation, and contact information of the various branches of the National Archives are available online at http://www.archives.gov/locations/ (see also Appendix E). While NARA's regional research centers maintain regular hours of operation, most of the branches recommend making an appointment prior to arrival to ensure that there will be space available in the reading room (reservations are not required at NARA's main facilities in Washington, D.C., and College Park, Maryland). By speaking with an archivist in advance, researchers can confirm that that branch of the National Archives has the materials the researchers plan to use. Many of the regional branches will also have the records pulled and ready for researchers prior to their arrival. Appendices C and D list the locations of all federal court records within the National Archives system.

The Federal Judicial History Office compiled this guide using a number of resources, starting with the National Archives' preliminary inventories and master location registers, the Library of Congress's online catalog and "American Memory" website, and several subscription databases, including HeinOnline, LexisNexis, Westlaw, America: History and Life, WorldCat, JSTOR, and ArchivesUSA. After conducting this preliminary research, the Federal Judicial History Office consulted the original records from many of the record groups described in this guide, as well as the published records related to the courts at the Law Library of Congress, the Library of the Supreme Court of the United States, and the library of the Administrative Office of the United States Courts.

This guide directs researchers to the variety of materials at NARA regarding the history of the federal courts, but it is not intended to replace the finding aids and inventories at the NARA facilities. Researchers will want to consult those more-detailed guides before examining the archival records of a court or federal agency. This guide also includes descriptions of the non-federal records that will be important sources of federal judicial history.

# Part I. Records of the Federal Judiciary

This section describes and directs researchers to the archival records and published decisions of courts and agencies that are or were part of the federal judiciary. A brief historical note precedes the description of the records in each section of this guide.

The official records of the U.S. courts are held almost exclusively by the National Archives and Records Administration (NARA). Chapter 1 discusses the records of the U.S. district and circuit courts, which are held in Record Group 21 at the regional branches of the National Archives and in the regional federal records centers. Chapter 2 describes the records of the U.S. courts of appeals in RG 276; these records are also held at NARA's regional facilities. Chapters 3 and 4 describe the records of the Supreme Court of the United States and the records of the federal courts of the District of Columbia, both of which are held at the National Archives in Washington, D.C. Chapter 5 examines the records of the federal courts of special jurisdiction, while Chapter 6 discusses records related to judicial administration of the federal courts. Most of the records described in Chapters 5 and 6 are held at the National Archives facilities in the Washington, D.C., area. Finally, Chapter 7 describes records of pre-federal, territorial, provisional, Confederate, and other non-Article III courts whose records are maintained within the National Archives system. Recently created judicial records, as well as some historic materials, are still maintained by the courts themselves and are usually available through the office of the clerk.

# Chapter 1. Records of the U.S. District and Circuit Courts

## A. Historical Note

From 1789 to 1911, two types of federal trial courts operated in most of the judicial districts throughout the nation. The Judiciary Act of 1789 established the U.S. district courts to serve as the federal trial courts for admiralty and maritime cases, as well as for some minor criminal cases and minor civil suits brought by the United States. The Act of 1789 established the U.S. circuit courts to serve as the federal trial courts for most federal crimes, for suits between citizens of different states, and for most causes initiated by the United States. Congress gave the circuit courts appellate jurisdiction over the final decrees of the district courts in admiralty and civil cases and the authority to entertain certain types of cases that were commenced in state courts. Although the U.S. district courts gradually gained greater jurisdictional authority, particularly in non-capital criminal cases, the U.S. circuit courts remained the more important trial courts through most of the nineteenth century.

The Judiciary Act of 1789 divided the United States into thirteen judicial districts and authorized the President, with the advice and consent of the Senate, to appoint a district judge to serve in each district. Congress also provided that two Supreme Court justices and the local district judge would serve as the judges of the circuit court in that district and that any two of those judges could convene the court. An act of 1793 provided that a single Supreme Court justice and the local district judge would serve as the judges of each circuit court.

The Judiciary Act of 1801 established separate judgeships to serve the circuit courts and relieved the Supreme Court justices of circuit-riding duties, but Congress repealed the Act and abolished the circuit judgeships in 1802. The Judiciary Act of 1802 reinstated the justices' circuit-riding responsibilities, but the Act authorized the district judge to convene a circuit court without the Supreme Court justice. In 1869, Congress created separate circuit judgeships to serve the circuit courts in each of the nine judicial circuits. The same act provided that a circuit court could be convened by the circuit judge, by the Supreme Court justice assigned to that circuit, by the district judge, or by any two of those judges.

In the original districts of Maine and Kentucky, and in many states newly admitted to the union during the nineteenth century, the U.S. district courts exercised the jurisdiction of a circuit court until the new district was incorporated into a judicial circuit. Appeals from such courts generally went to the Supreme Court of the United States and occasionally to the circuit court in another district within the state. Only in 1889 did Congress finally provide a circuit court for every judicial district in the nation and thus end the expanded jurisdiction of certain district courts.

In 1891, Congress transferred the appellate jurisdiction of the U.S. circuit courts to the newly created U.S. circuit courts of appeals. The Judicial Code of 1911 abolished the U.S. circuit courts, effective January 1, 1912, transferring their jurisdiction, pending cases, and records to the U.S. district courts, and making the district courts the sole trial courts of general jurisdiction in the federal judiciary.

## B. Records Description

Most of the historical records of the U.S. district courts and the U.S. circuit courts have been accessioned by the National Archives and Records Administration and are deposited in regional archives as part of Record Group 21. Unaccessioned historical records are located in the clerk's office of the respective district court or, in rare cases, at regional libraries and historical societies (see Appendix F for a list of federal court records held outside of the National Archives system).

The records in RG 21 are organized by judicial district, and thereunder by type of court (district and circuit). The records of each district and circuit court are then organized by the geographical divisions of that court, where applicable, and grouped therein by type of record or by the type of jurisdiction exercised by the court. The scope and organization of court records reflect the practices of the clerks who maintained them and vary considerably from court to court and across time.

Researchers interested in the history of a particular judicial district will need to examine the records of both the district and circuit courts of that district. Likewise, researchers interested in the work of a particular judge who served prior to the 1911 abolition of the circuit courts will want to review the records of both the district and circuit courts of the judicial district in which the judge served.

Most district and circuit court records fall into three basic categories: (1) general records, such as minute and docket books, describe the full scope of the courts' business and proceedings; (2) administrative records, which are sometimes designated the "records of the clerk of court," document the clerks' various responsibilities, such as the payment of expenses and the collection of fees, the operation of the jury system, and the admission of attorneys to practice before the court; and (3) case records, which detail the specific matters brought before the court.

The first two sections below describe the general and administrative records of the district and circuit courts together, since both types of courts kept similar types of records. Researchers should be mindful, however, that the district and circuit courts in a judicial district usually kept separate sets of general and administrative records. The third and fourth sections, on case records, discuss the case-related materials of the district and circuit courts separately since Congress assigned different jurisdiction to the district and circuit courts. The fifth section directs researchers to the published opinions of the district and circuit courts.

## C. General Records

Minute books, also known as journals, summarize the activities of each district and circuit court. Arranged chronologically, entries within the minutes describe the court's meeting place and the presiding judge or judges as well as the daily administrative functions of the court, including the adoption of procedural rules, the appointment of court officers, the summoning of grand and petit jurors, and the admission of attorneys to the bar. The minutes also describe the work and proceedings of the court in all of its areas of jurisdiction, including the dates that cases were heard, grand jury reports, jury findings and verdicts, court orders and judgments, sentences imposed, settlement agreements, and the postponement of cases. Some courts' general records include "rough" minutes, which are the volumes the clerk used to prepare the "final" or "engrossed" minutes. Many general court records also include minute books related to the selection of jury members.

District and circuit courts often kept various types of docket books, including judges' and clerks' dockets, issue dockets, "rough" dockets, motion dockets, subpoena dockets, writ execution dockets, grand jury dockets, judgment lien dockets, and dockets pertaining to specific areas of a court's jurisdiction. Docket books contain a chronological list of the proceedings held and papers filed in each case initiated in the court. Volumes correspond to particular years or court terms. Within each volume, cases are presented alphabetically or by case number. Each entry includes the case name and number, the names of the parties and their attorneys, abstracts of motions and orders, a record of fees charged and collected, the actions of U.S. marshals, and a statement of the court's disposition of the case. Jurisdictionally specific dockets may be stored with a court's general records, but those dockets are usually kept with the court's case records for the particular type of jurisdiction.

The general records of a court often include other volumes that document the proceedings of the court. Order, judgment, and decree books contain the text of each court's orders or judgments, as well as a record of the amount of monetary judgments, if any, in each case. Some order books contain the same information as minute books, and on rare occasions include verbatim transcripts of court proceedings. Final record books contain transcripts of papers submitted to and issued by the court in cases that were subsequently appealed.

The general records of a court may also include miscellaneous court papers, including caseload statistics kept by the court, rules, summonses, writs, lists of witnesses, miscellaneous or unidentified case papers, indexes to dockets or case files, affidavits, executions, copies of opinions, instructions to juries, bonds, judges' trial notes, rolls of attorneys, calendars, recognizances, and general correspondence.

Because the records within RG 21 reflect the individual filing system implemented by each court's clerks, some of the records filed under "General Records" in one court may be maintained with the case files or the clerks' records in another court.

## D. Administrative Records of the Clerk of Court

Although the Judiciary Act of 1789 authorized each district court to appoint a clerk to serve both the district and circuit courts of the district, the clerks generally maintained separate sets of records for the district and circuit courts. In 1839, Congress authorized the circuit courts to appoint their own clerks, but most circuit courts did not do so for several decades, and a few never did. In such cases, the clerk of the district court continued to serve as the clerk of the circuit court. The records of the clerks are generally included with the records of the district or circuit courts in which they served. Where a clerk served both the district and circuit courts of a district, the clerk's records for both courts may be filed with the records of the district court, but those records usually are maintained separately.

In addition to maintaining and preserving the records of the courts, clerks may have also performed administrative duties, including collecting fees from litigants, preparing the court's budget and managing its operating expenses, administering the jury system, recording the names of attorneys admitted to the bar, assigning cases and courtrooms to judges, and making the courts' rules of practice and procedure available to the public. On several occasions, Congress has also authorized the clerks to perform various other tasks, such as taking testimony or depositions in certain types of cases, preserving census returns and copyright materials, and transmitting naturalization papers to the Secretary of State.

The administrative records of a court help to outline both the individual responsibilities of the clerk and the larger workings of the court. Cash and fee books, ledgers, records of deposits to the U.S. Treasury, registries of funds, clerks' and marshals' account books, accounts of expenditures, reports to the commissioner of internal revenue, bills, receipts, and other accounting records all detail the financial operations of the courts. Other records relate to the daily functions of the court, including subpoenas, rules and procedures of the court, drafts of official forms, memorandum books, administrative orders, and reference calendars. Clerks also maintained docket and process books, including some kept specifically for the clerk or judge, as well as others that detailed the verdicts of the court or the actions and responsibilities of the marshal.

The clerks kept detailed records related to persons who worked or practiced in the court, including letters of appointment and lists of appointees, oaths of office for court employees, Civil War loyalty oaths for attorneys, rolls of attorneys admitted to practice, and bonds posted by court officers to secure the performance of their duties. Records related to witnesses and juries—including witnesses' affidavits and certificates of attendance, discharges of witnesses, jury attendance lists, grand jury reports, orders dismissing jurors, and jury books—are also kept among the clerks' papers. Other assorted papers, such as copyright registers, census schedules, deed books for forfeited lands, amnesty oaths for former Confederates, and the claims of election supervisors, may also be found among the papers of a clerk.

The administrative records of a court often include the official correspondence of the clerk and deputy clerks. During the nineteenth century, clerks frequently shared office space with the U.S. attorneys and marshals. For that reason, the official correspondence of the marshals and U.S. attorneys will occasionally be found among the records of a clerk. On rare occasions, the records of a clerk will also include the personal papers of the clerk or other court officials.

## E. U.S. District Courts: Case Records

The case records of the U.S. district courts are arranged into series according to the various types of jurisdiction exercised by the courts. Each district court series of case records contains case files and other jurisdictionally specific materials, including dockets, order and judgment books, and other documents related to that aspect of the courts' business. Case files contain the original papers submitted by the parties as well as other documents issued by the courts in those proceedings. The case files may also contain transcripts of testimony or exhibits introduced at trial, although the parties usually retained exhibits. Case files are arranged either chronologically by date of filing, numerically by case number, or in some cases, both chronologically and by case number. Case names and numbers can be found in docket books and related indexes. Within each case file, records may be organized in loose chronological fashion, by type of proceeding or document, or by some other method. Researchers can often trace the proceedings and outcome of a specific case either through entries in a docket book or by the endorsements made on a case file's outer jacket.

Each of the following subsections describes different types of case records that were generated by the U.S. district courts. While the organization of case materials varied from court to court, the following jurisdictional categories generally describe the ways that most clerks maintained district court records. The clerks' organizational systems have been largely preserved in Record Group 21 at the various regional branches of the National Archives.

### 1. Law, Equity, and Civil Records

Article III of the Constitution extends the judicial power of the federal courts "to all Cases, in Law and Equity, arising under this Constitution, the Laws of the United States, and Treaties made, or which shall be made, under their Authority," although the Eleventh Amendment (1795) excludes from this jurisdiction suits against a state by noncitizens of that state. In the Judiciary Act of 1789, Congress gave the U.S. district courts jurisdiction, concurrent with the U.S. circuit courts and state courts, over suits at common law that were brought by the United States and in which the matter in dispute was between $100 and $500.

The act gave the district courts exclusive original jurisdiction in "all suits against consuls or vice-consuls" except those involving crimes. The majority of nineteenth century law cases brought in the district courts were suits initiated by the United States to recover debts owed to the federal government. With the abolition of the circuit courts in 1911, the district courts' law docket expanded to include diversity cases as well as those raising federal questions.

In equity cases, Congress only granted the district courts authority to grant temporary injunctions when the circuit court was not available. Congress enacted several statutes in the nineteenth century permitting district judges to convene equity proceedings in certain types of bankruptcy and tax cases, but the district courts did not acquire full equity jurisdiction until the abolition of the circuit courts in 1911. Equity cases, which the Judiciary Act of 1789 defined as suits in which it was not possible for a "plain, adequate and complete remedy [to] be had at law," included patent and trademark infringements, copyright violations, the fraudulent conveyance of real or personal property, libel, defamation, fraudulent misrepresentation, and the threatened breach of a contract.

The district courts conducted both law and equity proceedings from 1912 until 1938, at which time the *Federal Rules of Civil Procedure* abolished the distinction between law and equity pleading in the federal courts, thereby consolidating what had been two separate dockets into one "civil" docket. In 1966, admiralty cases were also transferred to the district courts' civil dockets.

"Law Records," which are made up of civil cases seeking a remedy under either a federal statute or the common law, included records from suits brought by the United States to recover fines and other debts, actions arising from violations of customs and internal revenue laws, cases involving fugitive slaves, suits for trespass, real estate disputes, infringements of patents, conspiracies in restraint of trade, and damages for assault and battery. "Law Records" often include docket books and "rough" dockets, execution registers, writs, rule books, order books, final record books, indexes, and case files. Law case files include complaints and declarations, narratives of debt, defendants' answers, demurrers and rejoinders, summonses, affidavits, depositions, exhibits (which may include charts, maps, and figures), court orders, records related to the summoning of juries, judges' charges to juries, verdicts, judicial opinions, agreements between parties, warrants, subpoenas, writs, bonds, petitions for remission of fines, and reports of court costs. Some collections of "Law Records" also include subsets related to specific types of law cases, including Civil War claims, suits brought by election supervisors (also sometimes maintained as their own set of records, described below), National Bank Compromise cases during the Great Depression, cases regarding debts on bonds, and forfeiture and internal revenue cases (also sometimes maintained as their own set of records).

"Equity Records" (sometimes called "Chancery Records") consist of case files, minutes, dockets, order books, and miscellaneous records, such as records from ancillary bankruptcy proceedings and stenographer's minutes. Equity case files contain bills of complaint (sometimes called bills in equity or bills in chancery), defendants' answers and pleas for dismissal, summonses, pleas to jurisdiction, exhibits, briefs, depositions, lists of interrogatories, transcripts of testimony, subpoenas and attachments, affidavits, court orders and decrees, injunctions, and other miscellaneous papers. Exhibits in equity case files include letters of patent, contracts, financial and accounting records, receipts, meeting minutes, and motion pictures

As with other records in RG 21, district court law and equity records are organized according to the filing system of each court's respective clerk. Unlike other court records, however, there is more variety in the ways that law and equity records were maintained. Until 1938, most district courts maintained their "Law Records" and "Equity Records" on separate dockets. Other courts docketed their law and equity records together. In some districts, pre-1912 district court equity proceedings were included with the circuit court's equity records. Since 1938, most district courts, in accordance with the *Federal Rules of Civil Procedure*, have filed all of their civil litigation in one civil docket, although several district courts continued to number law and equity cases separately. Researchers will need to consult the National Archives' preliminary inventory for the records of each judicial district to determine how the records are organized. Post-1938 civil records contain the same types of materials as the pre-1938 law and equity records.

## 2. Criminal Records

The Judiciary Act of 1789 limited the criminal jurisdiction of the district courts to cases involving minor offenses against the United States. The act gave circuit courts jurisdiction over all other federal crimes, as well as concurrent jurisdiction with the district courts over the lesser ones. In 1842, Congress granted the district courts jurisdiction concurrent with the U.S. circuit courts over all noncapital crimes. With the abolition of the circuit courts, effective January 1, 1912, the district courts acquired exclusive original jurisdiction of all federal crimes.

Criminal case files contain the full range of documents used in the prosecution and defense of those tried for crimes in the federal courts, including indictments, pleas of defendants, nolle prosequis, recognizances, subpoenas, depositions, transcripts of testimony, warrants, briefs, applications for extradition, petitions for writs of habeas corpus, jury verdicts, sentences, lists of jurors, attachments for contempt, transcripts from dockets, petitions for the mercy of the court, motions to quash indictments, and papers related to witness fees. Researchers can often trace the proceedings and outcome of a case through the endorsements made throughout the case file or on the file's outer jacket. Case files vary in size and content, with some early ones containing so little documentation that it is impossible to determine what charges had been brought against the defendant.

Criminal case files are usually organized by session and then by case number (although some early case files are organized alphabetically). Docket and minute books offer supplementary information, including records of papers filed, information about who was present at various proceedings, and the outcomes of cases. The criminal records of some district courts also contain separate collections of order books, bail bonds, abstracts of cases files, name indexes, records and indexes of verdicts and sentences, and compilations of indictments and informations.

## 3. Habeas Corpus Records

The Judiciary Act of 1789 authorized the district courts, circuit courts, and the Supreme Court to issue writs of habeas corpus to inquire into the reasons for confinement of petitioners held under federal authority. A writ of habeas corpus, Latin for "you have the body," ordered a detaining officer to bring the petitioner before the court, where a judge would determine whether the detention was lawful. Congress expanded the scope of the federal judiciary's habeas jurisdiction in 1833 to include cases involving persons who were being sued, prosecuted, or imprisoned for acting in accordance with U.S. law; in 1842 to cases involving foreign citizens who had been arrested by state or federal officials for actions carried out under the authority of their home government; and in 1867 to persons who had been denied their federal constitutional rights within a state court system. In a few instances—most notably the Civil War-era habeas acts (1863 and 1866) and the "McCardle repealer"

(1869)—Congress temporarily limited the federal judiciary's habeas jurisdiction.

Case files, which vary widely in their content, may include petitions for writs, transcripts of hearings on those petitions, affidavits, subpoenas, writs of habeas corpus, respondents' returns, recognizances, orders of discharge, testimony, judges' opinions, requests for appeal, correspondence, and related papers. Case files are usually arranged in chronological order by date of petition or alphabetically by name of petitioner. Habeas dockets record the date and title of papers filed in habeas cases, the names of petitioners and their attorneys, and other information relating to the proceedings. Most district courts maintained habeas records as a distinct series within the records of the court, although habeas papers may also be found among a court's criminal case files.

## 4. Bankruptcy Records

### a. Historical Note

Article I of the Constitution authorizes Congress to establish "uniform Laws on the subject of Bankruptcies throughout the United States." In the nineteenth century, Congress adopted four major pieces of bankruptcy legislation, each giving original jurisdiction in bankruptcy cases primarily to the U.S. district courts. The first four bankruptcy laws—adopted in 1800, 1841, 1867, and 1898—were enacted following major financial crises, and all but the last was a temporary emergency measure. Thus, until 1898 the federal courts exercised bankruptcy jurisdiction for only short periods of time. The 1898 act remained on the books until 1978, when Congress overhauled the federal bankruptcy system by authorizing the appointment of bankruptcy judges within each federal judicial district.

The Bankruptcy Act of 1800 provided only for the involuntary bankruptcy of merchants. Under the Act, debts were discharged by commissioners of bankruptcy (initially appointed by the district judges, but changed to presidential appointment in April 1802) and assignees selected by the creditors. The 1800 Act gave limited jurisdiction to the circuit courts, allowing the creditors or the bankrupt's assignees to request a jury trial in the circuit court of the judicial district in which the debtor resided, but this jurisdiction was transferred to the district courts in 1802. Although the act of 1800 was set to expire in 1805, Congress repealed it in December 1803 because of dissatisfaction with the limited nature of the law, as well as corruption and excessive expenses involved in the proceedings.

Following the Panic of 1837, Congress in 1841 enacted a new bankruptcy law that permitted all debtors to file for voluntary bankruptcy. The act also authorized creditors to seek the involuntary bankruptcy of merchants, bankers, and other types of businessmen. Like the act of 1800, the 1841 law was administered by court-appointed commissioners and assignees, but if creditors blocked the discharge of a debt, the debtor could seek relief through a jury trial. Congress repealed the act of 1841 in March 1843, just thirteen months after it went into effect, in response to the widespread dissatisfaction of both debtors and creditors with various provisions of the law.

In 1867, Congress enacted the third national bankruptcy act, providing for court-appointed registers in bankruptcy to assist the district courts in administering bankruptcy cases and to make adjudications in uncontested cases. The act, which was intended to balance the interests of both debtors and creditors, allowed for both voluntary and involuntary bankruptcy filings for persons and corporations, but it grew increasingly unpopular because of the high court fees it allowed, and Congress repealed the act in 1878.

In 1898, Congress made all persons (both natural and artificial) eligible for involuntary bankruptcy except for wage earners, farmers, unincorporated companies, national banks, state-chartered banks, and a few types of corporations. Any natural born person could also file for voluntary bankruptcy. The Bankruptcy Act of 1898 created the office of "referee in bankruptcy." In the absence of a district judge, referees were authorized to exercise most of the powers of a court of bankruptcy, although a referee's decision was subject to review by a district judge.

The act of 1898 was superseded by the Bankruptcy Reform Act of 1978, which established separate courts of bankruptcy within each judicial district as adjuncts of the district courts. The 1978 act also created the office of U.S. bankruptcy judge. Incumbent referees became the first bankruptcy judges, and subsequent judges were to be appointed by the President. Since 1984, however, bankruptcy judges have been appointed by the courts of appeals. Bankruptcy jurisdiction still rests with the district courts, but the courts refer bankruptcy cases to the bankruptcy judges of their respective districts. The decisions of a bankruptcy judge may be reviewed by a district judge.

### b. Records

The records of bankruptcy proceedings in the district courts are organized by the statutes under which the proceedings were initiated. Recent records may still be in the possession of the appropriate clerk of court or at a federal records center pending transfer to one of NARA's regional branches. Unless sealed, such records are available to the public.

Case files typically contain petitions of bankruptcy filed by creditors or debtors, schedules of bankrupts' assets and debts, receipts for the publication of bankruptcy notices, warrants for the seizure of bankrupts' property, the names and addresses of creditors, notices to creditors, proofs of debt, creditors' bonds and affidavits, summonses, depositions, transcripts of testimony or proceedings, correspondence, court orders, and records from the sale of bankrupts' property. Depending on the act under which a bankruptcy proceeding was initiated, case files may also include schedules of secured and unsecured creditors, transcripts of commissioners' meetings, and the reports of commissioners and referees. Within each grouping by statutory authority, bankruptcy case files may be arranged numerically by case number or alphabetically by name of petitioner.

In addition to case files, bankruptcy records also often include commissioners' commissions, calendars, bonds, certificates of discharge, reports, decrees, bills, receipts for dividends, ledgers, minutes, orders and order books, registers of petitions filed, and docket books. Some courts also maintained indexes listing the names of each bankrupt in alphabetical order.

Recently, the National Archives created a new record group, RG 578 (Records of the United States Bankruptcy Courts), for the records of bankruptcy proceedings conducted under the 1978 act. Several of NARA's regional branches have begun transferring the records of these proceedings from Record Group 21 to Record Group 578. Researchers interested in post-1978 bankruptcy records will need to consult with an archivist at the regional facility to determine whether the needed records are in RG 21 or RG 578.

## 5. Naturalization Records

In 1790, Congress authorized every "common law court of record" in the United States to naturalize aliens seeking to become U.S. citizens. U.S. district judges shared the responsibility with U.S. circuit judges, as well as with state and local magistrates, to examine naturalization petitions and issue orders granting or denying citizenship applications. The district courts' duties in naturalization proceedings lasted until 1990, when Congress conferred sole naturalization authority upon the Attorney General; district judges, however, continue to preside over naturalization ceremonies for newly admitted citizens.

The naturalization records within the district court records of RG 21 include declarations of intention to become a citizen, petitions for naturalization, and copies of certificates of citizenship (or stubs from certificates). These documents, which are grouped together and organized by petition number, contain personal information about the applicant, renunciation of allegiance to any foreign state or power, and the court's order granting or denying the petition. The records of particular applicants can be located using alphabetically arranged indexes to naturalization records that are available onsite at the regional branches of the National Archives, as well as in various historical and genealogical publications.

Record Group 21 contains other records produced as a result of the district courts' naturalization work, including minutes containing the names of aliens taking the oath of allegiance, receipt books, copies of preliminary forms, court orders, petitions for transfer of jurisdiction, circulars from other government agencies instructing clerks of court in naturalization procedures, registries of aliens, correspondence, monthly reports from the clerks of court to the Immigration and Naturalization Service (INS), and some miscellaneous papers. In the early twentieth century, district courts began taking depositions from witnesses in support of an applicant's petition for citizenship. These depositions, as well as lists of interrogatories, are often found among a district court's naturalization papers. Record Group 21 also includes some case files from instances when the INS contested an alien's petition for citizenship. Naturalization case files include court orders, depositions, exhibits, findings of facts, conclusions of law, the recommendations of naturalization examiners, and declarations by petitioners. In a few rare instances, verbatim transcripts of court hearings have also been preserved in the records.

Some district courts kept separate files of notices of application for admission to citizenship, military petitions, women's petitions for repatriation after their foreign husband had died, applications for naturalization that had been refused by the court, petitions filed by U.S. attorneys to annul certificates of naturalization of immigrants who did not comply with federal naturalization laws, and various lists and court orders.

Prior to the Naturalization Act of 1906, each court used its own set of forms and procedures for the naturalization of aliens. Congress's creation of the Bureau of Immigration and Naturalization (and in 1933, the INS) brought uniformity to the naturalization process by authorizing federal officials in Washington to revise and distribute naturalization forms. The courts continued to naturalize aliens, but they no longer used their own forms. The 1906 act also ordered the courts to forward all forms dated after September 26, 1906, to the newly established bureau and to keep duplicates of all paperwork for their own records.

Records related to naturalization will also be found in Record Group 85, Records of the Immigration and Naturalization Service, which is held at the National Archives' various regional facilities. The naturalization records of some state and local courts are also included in RG 21 and RG 85.

### 6. Admiralty Records

Article III of the Constitution vests the federal courts with jurisdiction in all admiralty and maritime cases, and the Judiciary Act of 1789 granted the U.S. district courts exclusive original jurisdiction in such cases. Congress never defined the precise scope of the courts' admiralty jurisdiction, but the Supreme Court held in a series of nineteenth century decisions that the federal admiralty jurisdiction extended beyond the high seas to include the nation's publicly navigable rivers, bays, lakes, and canals. From 1789 until 1966, admiralty cases were governed by separate rules of procedure and were documented in a separate docket. In 1966, the *Federal Rules of Civil Procedure* were revised so that admiralty cases became part of the federal courts' civil docket (see above).

Admiralty proceedings could be *in rem*, meaning against "a thing," such as a ship or other property, or *in personam*, meaning against "an individual." Some admiralty suits involved the federal government, such as cases that arose from seizures for violations of customs laws or embargoes, or for illegal involvement in the slave trade. Other cases were brought between private parties, including suits to recover and establish title to ships, or actions involving prizes, ransom, and salvage. Admiralty dockets also contained a variety of maritime contract and tort cases, including suits involving seamen's wages, towage, stowage, wharfage, marine insurance, collisions, breach of contract, and injuries to persons and property sustained on any of the nation's navigable waters.

Admiralty case files include libels and informations (the instruments used to commence an action in admiralty), briefs, answers, subpoenas, interrogatories, correspondence regarding claims, summonses, attachments for condemnation of ships or property, agreements between parties to enter stipulations, defendants' answers to charges, rules of the court, court orders and decrees, bills, depositions and transcripts of oral testimony, reports of commissioners, petitions for remission of forfeited goods, and opinions of the court. Case files may also include exhibits, such as logbooks, crew lists, cargo manifests, citations, and arrest warrants. Related admiralty records include dockets, order books, surveys of ships and cargoes damaged on the high seas, marshals' vessel sale books, logs and registers relating to captured prize vessels, stipulations for costs and value, and bonds for costs on appeal.

### a. Prize Case Records

In several statutes adopted subsequent to the Judiciary Act of 1789, Congress confirmed that the district courts' admiralty jurisdiction included prize cases. From the sixteenth through the nineteenth centuries, governments at war often issued letters of marque, authorizing private ships to capture enemy vessels or merchant ships trading with the enemy. In the United States, the privateer would bring the captured ship, or "prize," to a federal district court, where a district judge would determine if the vessel had been a belligerent or involved in trade with the enemy. The court would condemn and order the sale of legally captured ships, with the proceeds given to the captor. If the vessel was found to have been neutral, however, the court would order the return of the ship and its cargo to its former owner. Prize decisions could be appealed to the circuit court and ultimately to the Supreme Court of the United States.

Records relating to prize cases, most of which arose during the War of 1812 and the Civil War, may be included within a court's admiralty records but are often maintained separately. Prize court records generally consist of (1) records generated by the courts and government officials in the process of determining the fate of each captured vessel and (2) documents seized on captured ships.

Prize records include docket books, depositions, motions, orders, decrees, briefs, notes for oral arguments, libels for condemnation, the reports of the prize commissioners, the prize commissioners' official correspondence, the U.S. marshals' accounts, and the opinions of the court. In some instances judges requested expert testimony, reports on navigation, or charts to illustrate the circumstances surrounding the capture. Claimants in each case also submitted exhibits to prove that a ship either was or was not engaged in lawful trade. Exhibits—including business letters, insurance policies, and affidavits—often detail business transactions between ship owners and both foreign and domestic firms.

Soon after being brought into port, a prize was placed into the custody of the U.S. marshal, who would take out insurance policies to protect the ship and its cargo against loss from fire or other damage. If the ship was in disrepair or its cargo was perishable, the marshal would put the prize up for auction. The court records document the insurance, advertisement, and sale of each prize.

Prior to the commencement of a prize case, a court-appointed prize commissioner prepared a report based on depositions he had taken from the captains, passengers, and crew. Each court adopted a series of standard interrogatories to be asked of all persons onboard the vessel in an effort to determine the history and status of the ship.

Documents seized on captured ships became part of the record of the court in prize cases. These include the ship's official papers (a register, enrollment, and license to engage in trade), lists of articles and crew lists, clearance papers, bills of health, receipts, invoices, logbooks, manifests, bills of lading, charters, bills, and insurance policies. Some case files also include the personal letters of the seamen or correspondence the ship was transporting for others.

### b. Confiscation Records

In July 1862, Congress adopted the Second Confiscation Act, permitting the seizure and condemnation of property owned by persons who were engaged in aiding the Confederate war effort. The proceedings would be *in rem*, meaning against "the thing," and could be initiated in any U.S. district court where the property was located or brought. Such property would be condemned and sold, with the proceeds deposited in the U.S. Treasury.

Confiscation records are usually maintained as a distinct series within the records of a district court, although they are sometimes grouped with other types of cases. Some courts docketed confiscation cases with prize cases, most likely because confiscation proceedings were patterned after admiralty proceedings, and also because prize and confiscation cases both involved the seizure of private property. Other courts filed confiscation cases with treason cases, most likely because the Second Confiscation Act also provided for criminal proceedings against accused traitors.

Confiscation case files include documents related to the ownership and seizure of the property, including orders of seizure, libels, decrees, petitions, advertisements for public sale and proofs of public notice, inventories of property seized, correspondence, and records from the sale. In addition to case files, a district court's confiscation records may include docket books, minutes, orders of seizure, trial records, and judgment dockets.

## 7. Records of the U.S. Commissioners

Throughout most of the nineteenth and twentieth centuries, commissioners assisted federal judges in the local enforcement of federal law. In 1793, Congress authorized judges of the U.S. circuit courts to appoint "discreet persons learned in the law" to take bail in federal criminal proceedings. In 1812, Congress expanded this authority to include the taking of affidavits and bail in civil cases. An Act of 1817 referred to these officers as "commissioners" and also gave them the authority to take depositions of witnesses for use in civil cases. In 1842, Congress granted commissioners further authority to arrest, imprison, and release on bail any persons accused of committing a federal crime.

Over the remainder of the nineteenth century, Congress periodically expanded the powers of commissioners to aid in the enforcement of specific federal laws. The Fugitive Slave Act of 1850 granted commissioners jurisdiction concurrent with that of federal judges to authorize the apprehension and trial of runaway slaves. The Civil Rights Act of 1866, which extended citizenship to former slaves, authorized commissioners to make arrests and institute proceedings against those who violated the constitutional rights of former slaves. And the Chinese Exclusion Acts of the 1880s gave commissioners the same authority as judges to order the removal of Chinese immigrants who were unlawfully in the United States.

In 1896, Congress established the formal office of U.S. commissioner and transferred the authority to appoint commissioners from the circuit courts to the judges of the district courts. In 1968, Congress replaced the office of U.S. commissioner with that of U.S. magistrate (changed to magistrate judge in 1990). In addition to creating the new title, the Federal Magistrates Act of 1968 also expanded the magistrates' authority to conduct misdemeanor trials with the consent of the defendants, to serve as special masters in civil actions, and to assist district judges in pretrial and discovery proceedings as well as appeals for post-trial relief. The 1968 act authorized a majority of district judges on any court to assign to magistrates "additional duties as are not inconsistent with the Constitution and laws of the United States."

The records of the U.S. commissioners are included with the records of the district court for the district they served. Commissioners' records consist primarily of criminal return dockets and the record of proceedings in criminal cases. Arranged chronologically within bound volumes, these records show the charges against defendants, the dates on which warrants and subpoenas were issued and returned, pleas entered, bonds posted, the names of witnesses and the dates they appeared before the commissioner, dates of imprisonment, rulings of the commissioner, and the commissioner's fees for hearing each case (commissioners remained on a fee system until 1968).

Additional records of the U.S. commissioners include other types of docket books, costs books, minutes of testimony taken, bail registers, depositions, recognizances, arrest warrants, orders, fee books, transcripts of proceedings in extradition cases, records of habeas corpus proceedings in cases involving Chinese aliens subject to deportation, vouchers, claims for fees, accounts, case files of cases that did not go to grand juries, lists of cases, affidavits, petitions, and proofs in fugitive slave cases. Some records from magistrates and magistrate judges, including order books and records of proceedings, continue to be accessioned with the records of the U.S. commissioners.

## 8. Fugitive Slave Records

In 1793, Congress empowered slave owners, or their agents and attorneys, to seize runaway slaves and bring them before a U.S. district or circuit judge (or a county or city magistrate) to determine whether the fugitive was the legal property of the claimant. If the judge determined that the captive was the claimant's slave, the court issued a certificate of ownership, authorizing the slaveholder to transport the slave back to the state or territory from which the slave had fled.

As one component of the Compromise of 1850, Congress enacted a new Fugitive Slave Act that conferred upon federal judges and commissioners the authority to issue warrants for the arrest of fugitive slaves, to conduct summary hearings for the purpose of determining the legal status of persons arrested under the act, and to issue certificates of ownership to successful claimants. The act permitted claimants to establish ownership by affidavit or deposition, but it forbade alleged fugitives from testifying on their own behalf. In addition, the statute made interfering with the enforcement of the act a crime cognizable in the U.S.

district courts, and it provided for the return of fugitive slaves at government expense if necessary to prevent rescue attempts. Congress repealed both fugitive slave laws on June 28, 1864.

Pre-1850 fugitive slave cases are usually found among a district court's Law Records (see above). Post-1850 records from fugitive slave cases are generally maintained as a distinct group within the records of a district court, although they are sometimes held within the records of a court's commissioners. Fugitive slave case files are arranged numerically (which is usually also by date filed) and contain affidavits and depositions submitted by claimants, warrants for the arrest of fugitive slaves, records of hearings to establish ownership, and accounts of expenses incurred by marshals in transporting, protecting, housing, feeding, and delivering fugitive slaves. Case files also often contain documentation from the petitioner's state or local court in support of ownership claims. In a few rare instances, case files also include transcribed testimony and judges' opinions.

Some clerks kept bound volumes of petitions filed under the Fugitive Slave Act of 1850. Arranged numerically by case, these volumes include copies of the documents that were filed in fugitive slave cases, including petitions of the alleged slave owners, physical descriptions of the fugitive slaves, ownership papers, affidavits, depositions, probate records, and court orders.

Records related to the enforcement of the fugitive slave acts will also be found in other federal court records, including the courts' general correspondence files and habeas corpus records. District court criminal case files often include case papers related to the rescue or harboring of fugitive slaves.

## 9. Records Concerning the Supervision of Elections

As part of its effort to protect voting rights in federal elections after the Civil War, Congress in 1871 enacted a statute requiring circuit judges, upon receipt of a written request, to appoint election supervisors to oversee the registration of voters and to monitor elections. The vast majority of election supervisors were appointed in southern states, where intimidation and voting irregularities were most prevalent. The statute was repealed in 1894.

The records of several U.S. district courts include a series of case files related to suits brought by election supervisors; some of these suits have to do with supervisors seeking compensation for their services. A limited number of case files may also be found among a district court's

Law Records (discussed above). Most of the records in RG 21 related to election supervisors, however, are maintained with the case records of the U.S. circuit courts (see below).

## F. U.S. Circuit Courts: Case Records

The case records of the U.S. circuit courts are organized into series according to the types of jurisdiction exercised by the courts. Each subset of case records contains case files and other jurisdictionally specific materials, including dockets, order and judgment books, and other documents related to that aspect of the courts' business. Case files contain the original papers submitted by the parties as well as other documents issued by the courts in those proceedings. Case files may also contain transcripts of testimony or exhibits introduced at trial, although the parties usually retained exhibits. Case files are arranged either chronologically by date of filing, numerically by case number, or in some cases, both chronologically and by case number. Case names and numbers can be found in docket books and related indexes. Within each case file, records may be organized in loose chronological fashion, by type of proceeding or document, or by some other method. Researchers can often trace the proceedings and outcome of a case either through entries in a docket book or by the endorsements made on a case file's outer jacket.

Each of the following subsections describes the different types of original and appellate jurisdiction case records that were generated by the U.S. circuit courts. While the organization of case materials varied from court to court, the following jurisdictional categories generally describe the ways that most clerks maintained circuit court records. As noted earlier, the clerks' organizational schemes have been largely preserved in Record Group 21 at the various regional branches of the National Archives.

### 1. Equity and Law Records

Article III of the Constitution extends the judicial power of the federal courts "to all Cases, in Law and Equity, arising under this Constitution, the Laws of the United States, and Treaties made, or which shall be made, under their Authority," although the Eleventh Amendment (1795) excludes from this jurisdiction suits against a state by noncitizens of that state. In the Judiciary Act of 1789, Congress gave circuit courts jurisdiction concurrent with state courts over common law and equity suits when the matter in dispute was valued at greater than $500 and the suit was brought by the United States, an alien, or a citizen of a state other than the one in which the suit was brought. The act of 1789 also granted circuit courts jurisdiction, concurrent with the district courts and the state courts, over suits at common law brought by the United States when the matter in dispute was valued at $100 to $500. "Law Records," which are made up of civil cases seeking a remedy under either a federal statute or the common law, included suits brought by the United States to recover fines and other debts, actions arising from violations of customs and internal revenue laws, cases involving fugitive slaves, trespasses, suits involving real estate disputes, infringements of patents, and conspiracies in restraint of trade. "Law Records" often include docket books and "rough" dockets, execution registers, writs, rule books, order books, final record books, indexes, and case files. Law case files include complaints and declarations, narratives of debt, defendants' answers, demurrers and rejoinders, summonses, affidavits, depositions, exhibits (which may include charts, maps, and figures), court orders, records related to the summoning of juries, judges' charges to juries, verdicts, judicial opinions, agreements between parties, warrants, subpoenas, writs, bonds, petitions for remission of fines, and reports of court costs. Some collections of "Law Records" also include subsets related to specific types of law cases, such as Civil War claims, suits brought by election supervisors (also sometimes maintained as their own set of records, described below), cases regarding debts on bonds, and internal revenue cases (also sometimes maintained as their own set of records).

Equity cases, which the Judiciary Act of 1789 defined as suits in which it was not possible for a "plain, adequate and complete remedy [to] be had at law," included patent and trademark infringements, copyright violations, the fraudulent conveyance of real or personal property, libel, defamation, fraudulent misrepresentation, and the threatened breach of a contract. "Equity Records" (sometimes called "Chancery Records") consist of case files, minutes, dockets, order books, and other miscellaneous records, such as records from ancillary bankruptcy proceedings and stenographer's minutes. Equity case files contain bills of complaint (sometimes called bills in equity or bills in chancery), defendants' answers and pleas for dismissal, summonses, pleas to jurisdiction, exhibits, briefs, depositions, lists of interrogatories, transcripts of testimony, subpoenas and attachments, affidavits, court orders and decrees, injunctions, and other miscellaneous papers. Exhibits in equity case files include letters of patent, contracts, financial and accounting records, receipts, meeting minutes, and motion pictures.

As with other records in RG 21, circuit court "law" and "equity" records are organized according to the filing system of each court's respective clerk. Unlike other types of case records, however, there is more variety in the ways that law and equity records were maintained. In most districts, the circuit courts' "Law Records" and "Equity Records" were maintained as distinct sets of records. Other courts docketed their law and equity records together. In several districts, the circuit court's law records were maintained with the circuit court's appellate records (to be discussed below). Researchers will need to consult the National Archives' inventory for the records of each judicial district to determine how the records are organized.

## 2. Criminal Records

The Judiciary Act of 1789 gave the U.S. circuit courts original jurisdiction over all federal crimes (this jurisdiction was concurrent with the district courts in cases involving lesser federal offenses). From 1879 until the establishment of the circuit courts of appeals in 1891, the circuit courts also heard appeals from the district courts in criminal cases in which the sentence was imprisonment or a fine of more than $300. (With the abolition of the circuit courts, effective January 1, 1912, the district courts acquired exclusive original jurisdiction in all federal criminal cases.)

Criminal case files contain the full range of documents used in the prosecution and defense of those tried for crimes in the federal courts, including indictments, pleas of defendants, nolle prosequis, recognizances, subpoenas, depositions, transcripts of testimony, warrants, briefs, applications for extradition, petitions for writs of habeas corpus, jury verdicts, sentences, lists of jurors, attachments for contempt, transcripts from dockets, petitions for the mercy of the court, motions to quash indictments, presidential pardons, and witness fees. Researchers can often trace the proceedings and outcome of a case through the endorsements made throughout the case file or on the file's outer jacket. Case files vary in size and content, with some early ones containing so little documentation that it is impossible to know what charges had been brought against the defendant.

Criminal case files are usually organized by session and then by case number (although some early case files are organized alphabetically). Dockets, minutes, and final record books offer supplementary information, including records of papers filed, information about who was present at various proceedings, and the outcomes of cases.

Records of appeals in criminal cases from the district to the circuit courts are grouped with the circuit courts' appellate records, which are described below.

### 3. Habeas Corpus Records

The Judiciary Act of 1789 authorized the district courts, circuit courts, and the Supreme Court to issue writs of habeas corpus to inquire into the reasons for confinement of petitioners held under federal authority. A writ of habeas corpus, Latin for "you have the body," ordered a detaining officer to bring the petitioner before the court, where a judge would determine whether the detention was lawful. Congress expanded the scope of the federal judiciary's habeas jurisdiction in 1833 to include cases involving persons who were being sued, prosecuted, or imprisoned for acting in accordance with U.S. law; in 1842, to cases involving foreign citizens who had been arrested by state or federal officials for actions carried out under the authority of their home government; and in 1867, to persons who had been denied their federal constitutional rights within the state court systems. In a few instances—most notably the Civil War-era habeas acts (1863 and 1866) and the "McCardle repealer" (1869)—Congress temporarily limited the federal judiciary's habeas jurisdiction.

Case files, which vary widely in their content, may include petitions for writs, transcripts of hearings on those petitions, affidavits, subpoenas, writs of habeas corpus, respondents' returns, recognizances, orders of discharge, testimony, judges' opinions, requests for appeal, and related papers. Case files are arranged in chronological order by date of petition, or alphabetically by name of petitioner. Habeas dockets record the date and title of papers filed in habeas cases, the names of petitioners and their attorneys, and other information relating to the proceedings. Most circuit courts maintained habeas records as a distinct series within the records of a court, but habeas papers may also be found among a court's criminal case files.

### 4. Naturalization Records

In 1790, Congress authorized every "common law court of record" in the United States to naturalize aliens seeking to become U.S. citizens. U.S. circuit judges shared the responsibility with U.S. district judges, as well as with state and local magistrates, to examine naturalization petitions and issue orders granting or denying citizenship applications. The circuit courts performed these duties until those courts were abolished as of January 1, 1912. Most NARA regional archives maintain naturalization records with the records of the court to which the individual applied for citizenship, but some archives have merged naturalization records from the district and circuit courts.

The naturalization records within Record Group 21 include declarations of intention to become a citizen, petitions for naturalization, and duplicates or stubs of certificates of citizenship. These documents, which are grouped together and organized by petition number, contain personal information about the applicant, renunciation of allegiance to any foreign state or power, and the court's order granting or denying the petition. The records of particular applicants can be located using alphabetically arranged indexes to naturalization records that are available onsite at the regional branches of the National Archives, as well as in various historical and genealogical publications.

Record Group 21 contains other records produced as a result of the courts' naturalization work, including minutes that recorded the names of aliens taking the oath of allegiance, receipt books, copies of preliminary forms, orders of the court, petitions for transfer of jurisdiction, circulars from other government agencies instructing clerks of court in naturalization procedures, registries of aliens, correspondence, and other miscellaneous papers. In the early twentieth century, the courts began taking depositions from witnesses in support of an applicant's petition for citizenship. These depositions, as well as lists of interrogatories, are often found among a circuit court's naturalization papers. Record Group 21 also includes some case files from instances in which the United States contested the naturalization of petitioners. Circuit court naturalization case files include declarations of intention, depositions, correspondence, and annotations denoting the outcome of each case.

Prior to the Naturalization Act of 1906, each court used its own set of forms and procedures for the naturalization of aliens. With that Act, Congress created the Bureau of Immigration and Naturalization, which brought uniformity to the naturalization process by authorizing federal officials in Washington to revise and distribute naturalization forms. The courts continued to naturalize aliens, but they no longer used their own forms. The 1906 act also ordered the courts to forward all forms dated after September 26, 1906, to the newly established bureau, and to keep duplicates of all paperwork for their own records.

Records related to naturalization will also be found in Record Group 85 (Records of the Immigration and Naturalization Service), which is held at the National Archives' various regional facilities. The naturalization records of some state and local courts are also included in RG 21 and RG 85.

## 5. Bankruptcy Records

The federal bankruptcy laws of 1800, 1841, 1867, and 1898 gave jurisdiction in bankruptcy proceedings primarily to the U.S. district courts (see Chapter 1, section E.4, above). In a few instances, however, these acts gave limited jurisdiction to the circuit courts. The act of 1800 allowed creditors or the bankrupt's assignees to request a jury trial in the circuit court of the district in which the debtor resided, although this jurisdiction was transferred to the district courts in 1802. It is not likely that many, if any, circuit court records survive from cases brought under the 1800 act. The bankruptcy acts of 1841 and 1867 also authorized the circuit courts to hear certain bankruptcy cases in equity. The records and proceedings of these cases are usually maintained with the circuit courts' "Equity Records" (discussed above).

## 6. Records of the U.S. Commissioners

Although the U.S. commissioners assisted both the district and the circuit courts, and circuit courts appointed commissioners until 1896, the commissioners' records are usually held with the records of the district court for the district in which they served.

## 7. Fugitive Slave Records

In 1793, Congress empowered slave owners, or their agents and attorneys, to seize runaway slaves and bring them before a U.S. district or circuit judge (or a local magistrate) to determine whether the fugitive was the legal property of the claimant. If the judge determined that the captive was the claimant's slave, the court issued a certificate of ownership, authorizing the slaveholder to transport the slave back to the state or territory from which the slave had fled.

As one component of the Compromise of 1850, Congress enacted a new Fugitive Slave Act that conferred upon federal judges and commissioners the authority to issue warrants for the arrest of fugitive slaves, to conduct summary hearings for the purpose of determining the legal status of persons arrested under the act, and to issue certificates of ownership to successful claimants. The act permitted claimants to establish ownership by affidavit or deposition, but it forbade alleged fugitives from testifying on their own behalf. In addition, the statute made interfering with the enforcement of the act a crime cognizable in the U.S. district courts, and it provided for the return of fugitive slaves at government expense if necessary to prevent rescue attempts. Congress repealed both fugitive slave laws on June 28, 1864.

Pre-1850 fugitive slave cases are usually found in a circuit court's "Law Records" (see above). Post-1850 records from fugitive slave cases are generally maintained as a distinct group within the records of a circuit court, although they are sometimes held within the records of a court's commissioners (which are usually held with the records of the district court for that district). Fugitive slave case files are arranged numerically (which is usually also by date filed) and contain affidavits and depositions submitted by claimants, warrants for the arrest of fugitive slaves, records of hearings to establish ownership, and accounts of expenses incurred by marshals in transporting, protecting, housing, feeding, and delivering fugitive slaves. Case files also often contain documentation from the petitioner's state or local court in support of ownership claims. In a few rare instances, case files also include transcribed testimony and judges' opinions.

Some clerks of court kept bound volumes of petitions filed under the Fugitive Slave Act of 1850. Arranged numerically by case, these volumes include copies of the documents filed in a fugitive slave case, including petitions of the alleged slave owners, physical descriptions of the fugitive slaves, titles, affidavits, depositions, deeds, probate records, and court orders.

Records related to the enforcement of the fugitive slave acts will also be found in other federal court records, including the courts' general correspondence files and habeas corpus records. Case papers related to the rescue or harboring of fugitive slaves are usually found among the district courts' criminal case files, not the circuit courts'.

## 8. Records Concerning the Supervision of Elections

As part of its effort to protect voting rights in federal elections after the Civil War, Congress in 1871 enacted a statute requiring circuit judges, upon receipt of a written request, to appoint election supervisors to oversee the registration of voters and to monitor elections. In making these appointments, circuit judges were to consider the recommendations of the chief election supervisors, one of whom was appointed in each judicial district by the circuit courts. The statute was repealed in 1894. The vast majority of election supervisors were appointed in southern states, where intimidation and voting irregularities were most prevalent.

Circuit court records relating to the supervision of elections include records related to the appointment of commissioners as well as records related to the supervision of specific elections. Appointment records include letters of recommendation, minutes of special court sessions convened for the purpose of making appointments, certificates of appointment, oaths of service, forms relating to the qualifications of election supervisors, and financial accounts. Records related to the supervision of elections include petitions submitted by citizens, correspondence, lists of supervisors, sets of instructions to supervisors, poll books and election returns, lists of denied voters, affidavits, transcripts of testimony, and registers of voters. Records related to the supervision of elections are usually maintained as their own series of records, although in some districts they are held within the records of the clerk of the circuit court.

## 9. Appellate Records

The Judiciary Act of 1789 authorized the circuit courts to hear appeals from the district courts in admiralty cases where the amount in controversy exceeded $300, and in civil suits where the amount in dispute exceeded $50. This jurisdiction was expanded in 1803, when Congress lowered the monetary threshold for all appeals to $50. The bankruptcy acts of 1800, 1841, and 1867 gave the circuit courts appellate jurisdiction in bankruptcy cases, and in 1879 Congress authorized appeals from the district to the circuit courts in criminal cases in which the sentence was imprisonment or a fine of more than $300. In 1891, Congress transferred the circuit courts' appellate jurisdiction to the newly created courts of appeals.

Appeals from the district courts could be initiated either by a writ of appeal or a writ of error. A writ of appeal asked the circuit court to review both the law and the facts of the case, while a writ of error subjected only the legal issues to examination by the circuit court. Appeals in admiralty were by writ of appeal, while appeals in civil cases proceeded by a writ of error. Circuit court appellate records in Record Group 21 may appear under several different headings, including "Appellate Jurisdiction Records" and "Error and Appeal Records."

Appellate records generally include only dockets and case files, although some courts maintained separate collections of bonds, admiralty minutes, and other miscellaneous records. Several courts also filed their bankruptcy, admiralty, and civil appeals cases separately.

Appellate case files vary in size and scope depending on the type of case. Some case files consist of only a copy of the district court's proceedings, while others include copies of the papers filed in the case at the district level and copies of the district court's minute book entries pertaining to the case. Cases that involved the seizure of ships or violation of customs laws also often include copies of depositions and ships' papers (as described in the district court case records section of this chapter). Finally, case files may also contain briefs, writs of error and appeal, bills of exception, petitions for reversal or modification of the decrees of the district court, orders of the circuit court, assignments of error to rulings of the district court, judicial opinions, and Supreme Court mandates in cases appealed from the circuit court.

## G. Published Decisions

For the first century of the federal courts, there was no standard procedure for the reporting of lower federal court cases. Most district and circuit court decisions went unreported, and those that were reported appeared in privately published reports (often called nominative reports because they were named for the individuals who compiled and edited them) that generally focused on a particular court, judge, or type of law (such as admiralty, prize, railroad, bankruptcy, or patent law). Many federal court decisions were also printed in newspapers, journals, state reporters, and legal digests.

In the 1890s, the West Publishing Company collected the decisions from the nominative reports and published them along with many unreported district and circuit court decisions that the company acquired from judges, clerks of court, the Patent Office, newspapers, law journals, and other individuals. The resulting 30-volume *Federal Cases* (St. Paul, Minn.: West Publishing Co., 1894–1897), contains more than 20,000 cases argued and determined in the U.S. district and circuit courts from 1789 to 1880. In compiling the reports for *Federal Cases*, West's editors strove to "preserve everything of importance, and no effort has been spared to make the reports of these cases full and complete in every respect." A list of the sources they consulted appears in Volume 1 (pp. xxxvii–xlvii), and a bibliographic description of each source is included in Volume 30 (pp. 1261–84).

The cases in *Federal Cases* are arranged alphabetically by title and are then numbered consecutively (these numbers do not correspond with case numbers that will be found in the original case files or docket books at the National Archives; the numbers are merely intended to allow for easy cross-referencing within the 30 volumes of *Federal Cases*). Because some of these cases were originally reported in more than one source, with occasional variations in text or inclusion of different supplementary materials, the editors of *Federal Cases* selected what they judged to be the "best report of each case." In most cases, the editors used brackets and footnotes to insert additional material that did not appear in the version they had selected for publication.

In 1880, West began publishing the current decisions of the district and circuit courts in the *Federal Reporter* (St. Paul, Minn.: West Publishing Co., 1880–1925 [300 vols.]; second series, 1925–1993 [999 vols.]). Like the nominative reports that preceded it, the *Federal Reporter* was published privately rather than by the federal government, but West quickly developed a relationship with the district and circuit courts, from which it regularly received the courts' written decisions and stenographers' reports of oral opinions.

Over time, the scope of the *Federal Reporter* was broadened to include the decisions of other federal courts. So in 1933, West introduced the *Federal Supplement* (St. Paul Minn.: West Publishing Co., 1933–1998), which reported the decisions of the district courts and court of claims. The *Federal Supplement* grew to 999 volumes by 1998, at which time West introduced the *Federal Supplement, Second Series* (St. Paul, Minn.: West Publishing Co., 1998–), in which are reported the decisions of the district courts, as well as those of the U.S. Court of International Trade and the Judicial Panel on Multidistrict Litigation.

Opinions of the district courts interpreting the *Federal Rules of Civil Procedure* and the *Federal Rules of Criminal Procedure* are published in *Federal Rules Decisions* (St. Paul, Minn.: West Publishing Co., 1941–) and *Federal Rules Service* (Chicago: Callaghan and Co., 1939–1991; Rochester, N.Y.: Lawyer's Cooperative Publishing Co., 1991–1997; St. Paul, Minn.: West Publishing Co., 1997–). In addition to the opinions of the district courts, the latter series also reports other federal courts' decisions construing the *Federal Rules of Appellate Procedure*.

Decisions of the bankruptcy courts that were established by the Bankruptcy Reform Act of 1978 and certain decisions of the district courts involving bankruptcy issues are published in *Bankruptcy Reporter* (St. Paul, Minn.: West Publishing Co., 1980–) rather than in the *Federal Supplement*. The *Bankruptcy Reporter* also contains decisions of the Supreme Court and the U.S. courts of appeals dealing with bankruptcy matters.

Most of the decisions of the district courts are "unpublished" and do not appear in any published reporter. Because of the sheer volume of judicial opinions rendered annually, West seeks to publish only those opinions that "deal with issues of first impression," "establish, alter, modify or explain a rule of law," review or criticize an existing law, involve "unique factual situations," "present a unique holding," or "involve newsworthy events." Some unpublished opinions are reported by other commercial services and in topical reporters such as *Copyright Law Decisions* (New York: Commerce Clearing House, 1978–), *United States Patents Quarterly* (Washington, D.C.: Bureau of National Affairs, 1929–), and *U.S. Tax Cases* (New York: Commerce Clearing House, 1937–). Published and unpublished decisions are also available through electronic databases such as LexisNexis (at http:www.lexis.com) and Westlaw (at http://www.westlaw.com).

Researchers can follow the proceedings of a particular federal court through historic newspapers and periodicals. Local newspapers often reported the local district and circuit courts' dockets and the outcomes of important cases. Newspapers also often gave detailed descriptions of courtroom scenes and judicial opinions in high-profile cases. The recent digitization of many historic newspapers facilitates keyword searches for court-related articles.

Throughout the eighteenth and nineteenth centuries, lawyers often paid to have their oral arguments published in pamphlet form. Judges also often made their opinions and grand jury charges available for publication. In some rare instances—usually high profile cases—transcripts of entire judicial proceedings in particular cases were published in book form. Researchers may be able to locate such pamphlets and books by searching library catalogs or online databases like WorldCat and Google-Books.

# Chapter 2. Records of the U.S. Courts of Appeals

## A. Historical Note

The U.S. courts of appeals were the first federal courts designed exclusively to hear cases on appeal from trial courts. In an effort to relieve the caseload burden in the Supreme Court and to handle a dramatic increase in federal filings, Congress, in the Judiciary Act of 1891, established nine courts of appeals, one for each judicial circuit. The Act designated the existing circuit judges and a newly authorized judge in each circuit as the judges of the appellate courts. The circuit justice and district judges in the circuit also were authorized to sit on the three-person courts of appeals panels, but district judges were prohibited from considering appeals of their own decisions.

The act of 1891, commonly known as the Evarts Act, gave the U.S. courts of appeals jurisdiction over the great majority of appeals from the U.S. district and circuit courts. The act sharply limited the categories of cases that could be routinely appealed to the Supreme Court, and the Judiciary Act of 1925 and later statutes continued that trend while expanding the jurisdiction of the courts of appeals. By the 1930s, the courts of appeals also had jurisdiction over administrative appeals of decisions rendered by federal regulatory agencies.

The Evarts Act authorized each of the new courts to review the final decisions and certain interlocutory orders or decrees of the district courts in their circuit, except in cases for which direct review by the Supreme Court was statutorily provided. The act also conferred upon the new courts a limited original jurisdiction to issue writs necessary for the exercise of its primary appellate jurisdiction. The decisions of the courts of appeals were usually final in admiralty, diversity, patent, revenue, and criminal cases, although the Supreme Court was authorized to grant appeals in such cases. Congress preserved a right of appeal to the Supreme Court in all other cases where the amount in controversy exceeded $1,000.

Throughout the twentieth century, Congress altered and expanded the jurisdiction of the courts of appeals by reducing the categories of cases that could be routinely appealed to the Supreme Court and thus making court of appeals decisions final in those cases. Congress also granted the courts of appeals the authority to review the decisions of federal administrative agencies, such as the Federal Trade Commission, the National Labor Relations Board, the Securities and Exchange Commission, and the Federal Communications Commission.

The number and size of the courts of appeals grew in response to the addition of new states and territories as well as the increase in the number of cases appealed from the federal trial courts. In 1893, Congress established the Court of Appeals of the District of Columbia to hear appeals from the Supreme Court of the District of Columbia. In 1929, Congress created a court of appeals for the newly established Tenth Circuit. The U.S. courts of appeals for the Eleventh and Federal Circuits were established in 1980 and 1982, respectively. The latter is the only U.S. court of appeals with national jurisdiction. It hears appeals in patent cases and in cases decided by the U.S. Court of International Trade and the U.S. Court of Federal Claims. It also hears appeals of decisions of the Merit Services Protection Board and of various executive branch administrative decisions as designated by law.

By 1922, there were at least three circuit judges assigned to each court of appeals, obviating the regular service of district judges on the courts' panels. In the 1930s, as the number of circuit judges on the courts of appeals increased beyond three, several of the courts increased the size of their panels in important cases and in those in which there was a significant split of opinion among the judges. The Supreme Court sanctioned these "*en banc* hearings" in 1941. The Judicial Code of 1948 authorized such hearings upon the vote of the majority of a court's active judges.

In 1948, Congress changed the name of each circuit court of appeals to the U.S. Court of Appeals for the respective circuit.

## B. Records Description

The historical records of the twelve regional U.S. courts of appeals have been accessioned by the National Archives and Records Administration (NARA) and are deposited at its regional branches as part of Record Group 276. Newer records are located in the offices of the respective clerks of court, in the circuit libraries, or in one of the federal records centers. The records of the U.S. Court of Appeals for the Federal Circuit have not yet been accessioned by NARA. Once accessioned, these records will make up Record Group 504 at the National Archives in Washington, D.C. The records of the U.S. courts of appeals are made up of general and administrative records, as well as case materials.

## C. General and Administrative Records

Each U.S. court of appeals maintained a general record of its proceedings in its minutes and dockets. Minute books (sometimes called journals or court record books) provide a daily account of the business of each court of appeals. Arranged chronologically by court session, entries in the minutes indicate the judge or judges presiding on certain days, the matters before the court and the actions taken on those matters, the attorneys making appearances, the adoption of procedural rules, the appointment of court officers, and the admission of attorneys to practice.

Dockets, which correspond to particular years or terms of court, contain a chronological summary of the proceedings and filings in each matter before a court of appeals. Within each box or volume, cases are presented alphabetically or by case number. Entries indicate case titles and numbers, the name of the lower court or commission from which each case was appealed, the nature and date of the rulings, the names of the parties and their attorneys, the dates of specific actions and filings, and, when applicable, citations to subsequent proceedings. Dockets also contain abstracts of papers filed with the court, summaries of the court's orders and other actions, and notations indicating fees charged by the court. More recent dockets may also include information regarding exhibits or legal precedents alluded to in a case.

Some courts kept additional dockets that dealt with specific types of matters. "Leave Dockets" listed all of the petitions received by the court, such as petitions seeking changes of venue in the district court or requests for the issuance of various writs. Most petitions in a leave docket were denied. "Miscellaneous Dockets" kept a record of cases that were part of the courts' original jurisdiction, including petitions for writs, requests for injunctions or restraining orders, and motions to stay court orders or vacate sentences. Some courts also preserved "clerk's memorandum books" and "rough dockets," which were the clerk's working dockets while cases were before the court.

Many courts maintained lists of appellants and appellees in bound volumes or card files. Indexes in bound volumes generally indicated only case names and numbers, but card files may also include information regarding the issues or subject matter of the case, the actions of the court, references to other cases, and citations to the *Federal Reporter*.

The administrative records of an appeals court may include fee books, correspondence between judges and clerks, letters received from the public, and memorials issued upon the death of judges, court officers, and prominent local attorneys. Some courts also kept "Designation Files," which consist of forms filed when circuit judges were assigned to sit in another judicial circuit or in a specific district court case.

Many of the administrative records of a court of appeals pertain to attorneys who practiced before the court. These records include attorney admission files, rolls and indexes of attorneys admitted to practice, and records related to disbarment. Attorney admission files include motions for admission to the bar, personal statements of applicants, character reports issued by bar examiners, letters of reference, statements from the clerks of other courts confirming that the applicant is a member of the bar in good standing, questionnaires, affidavits, and certificates of admission. Disbarment files include correspondence, court orders of disbarment, reports and charges by a court's grievance committee, exhibits, respondent's answers to court rulings, and petitions for reinstatement.

## D. Case Records

Court of appeals case records generally consist of three types of records: (1) transcripts of the official record from the lower court or federal agency, including printed copies of the proceedings of the trial or hearing as well as copies of papers that were filed in the trial; (2) documents submitted to the court of appeals by the parties, including briefs, appendices, petitions, and answers; and (3) papers produced during the appellate proceedings, including stipulations, agreements, motions, correspondence between the court and the parties, judgments, orders, decrees, mandates sent to district courts or received from the Supreme Court, and judicial opinions.

The organization of court of appeals case records varies significantly from court to court. Some clerks collected all of the various materials related to specific cases into "case files." Other courts filed the three types of case records listed above as distinct sets of records. Whether stored in integrated case files or by type of record, court of appeals case records are arranged by case number, which may be obtained from a court's alphabetically arranged indexes or docket.

Several courts of appeals separated matters related to the courts' original jurisdiction (such as the review of decisions by federal agencies or commissions, petitions for various writs or rehearings, and motions to vacate sentences or stay court orders) from the court's appellate jurisdiction records. Some courts also set apart materials from certain types of cases—patent or desegregation cases, for example—from their general case papers.

Many courts maintained copies of judicial opinions in loose files or in bound volumes. Arranged by court term and thereunder either by case number or alphabetically by case name, opinions provide a summary of the facts of the case and the reasons for the court's decision. Some courts also kept bound volumes of handwritten opinions and mandates of the courts.

## E. Published Decisions

From their establishment in 1891, the courts of appeals issued their decisions in the form of written opinions, which the West Publishing Company included in the *Federal Reporter* (St. Paul, Minn.: West Publishing Co., 1880–1925), a series of 300 volumes that had originally only reported the decisions of the district and circuit courts. In 1925, West introduced the *Federal Reporter, Second Series* (St. Paul, Minn.: West Publishing Co., 1925–1993) to report the decisions of the courts of appeals (along with those of the district courts, until 1933, when West began publishing district court opinions in the *Federal Supplement*).

In 1964, the Judicial Conference of the United States resolved that district and appeals court judges ought to "authorize the publication of only those opinions which are of general precedential value" and that published opinions "be succinct." Despite the ensuing trend toward the selective publication of opinions, the total number of reported court of appeals opinions continued to grow with the increase in the size of the courts' dockets. After the *Federal Reporter, Second Series* grew to 999 volumes in 1993, West introduced the *Federal Reporter, Third Series* (St. Paul, Minn.: West Publishing Co., 1993–).

Each court of appeals has adopted a set of rules, procedures or policies for determining which opinions will be officially "published" in the *Federal Reporter*. Generally, an opinion must have "precedential value" in order to be selected. Since the mid-twentieth century, several private companies have printed "unpublished" appeals court decisions in topical reporters, and beginning in 2001, decisions not selected for publication in the *Federal Reporter* have been printed in West's *Federal Appendix* (St. Paul, Minn.: West Publishing Co., 2001–).

Until 2006, each of the circuits adopted its own rules regarding whether "unpublished" opinions (meaning those not included in the *Federal Reporter*) could be cited in current proceedings. Some courts allowed the citation of "unpublished" opinions while others courts discouraged or prohibited their use. In 2006, an amendment to the *Federal Rules of Appellate Procedure*, Rule 32.1, required courts of appeals to permit "unpublished" or "nonprecedential" opinions to be cited.

Except for a brief period from 1891 until 1899, when Samuel A. Blatchford compiled 63 volumes of *United States Courts of Appeals Reports* (New York: Banks and Brothers, 1893–1899), and from 1982 to 1995, when the Court of Appeals for the Federal Circuit officially reported its opinions in thirteen volumes of *Cases Decided in United States Court of Appeals for the Federal Circuit* (Washington, D.C.: G.P.O., 1985–2000), West has been the exclusive reporter and publisher of the decisions of the U.S. courts of appeals. The published decisions of the Court of Appeals for the District of Columbia are described in Chapter 4.

# Chapter 3. Records of the Supreme Court of the United States

## A. Historical Note

Article III of the Constitution places the judicial power of the federal government in "one supreme Court, and in such inferior Courts" as Congress might decide to establish. The Constitution granted the Supreme Court original jurisdiction in cases in which states were a party and in cases involving diplomats, but left for Congress to determine the size, appellate jurisdiction, and other responsibilities of the Court. The Judiciary Act of 1789 established a Supreme Court with one chief justice and five associate justices. The act further defined the jurisdiction of the Court to include appellate jurisdiction in larger civil cases and cases in which state courts ruled on the constitutionality of federal statutes. The act also authorized the Court to appoint a clerk to record its proceedings, filings, decrees, judgments, and determinations.

The 1891 act establishing the circuit courts of appeals restricted the right of automatic appeal to the Supreme Court by giving the justices authority to grant review through certiorari. At the same time, it gave the courts of appeals the authority to certify specific questions for appeal to the high court. The Judges' Bill of 1925 further increased the justices' discretion in determining what cases to hear, and in 1988 Congress eliminated nearly all of the Supreme Court's mandatory jurisdiction. Since 1891, the majority of cases before the Court have been appeals from state and federal court decisions interpreting the Constitution, federal statutes, and treaties. The most common actions invoking the Supreme Court's original jurisdiction are petitions for writs of mandamus and prohibition, and suits involving boundary and water rights disputes between states.

## B. Records Description

The historical records of the Supreme Court make up Record Group 267 at the National Archives in Washington, D.C. Record Group 267 contains general records, case records, the records of the clerk, and the records of the marshal of the Supreme Court. Nontextual records, including sound recordings, are held at the National Archives at College Park, Maryland.

## C. General Records

The general records of the Supreme Court describe the full scope of the Court's business and proceedings. These records include minutes and dockets, as well as opinions, indexes, memorandums, transcripts and recordings of oral arguments, correspondence, and other miscellaneous items.

The records of the Supreme Court include both rough and engrossed minutes. Minutes indicate the Court's meeting place, the names of the justices and Court officers who were present at each session, the swearing in of new justices, the admission of attorneys to practice, the resignation and appointment of Court officers, the names of cases and of the attorneys appearing before the Court, memorial proceedings for deceased justices and other prominent persons, the adoption of procedural rules, and the decisions and orders of the Court. Since 1890, the Court has published bound *Journals* that contain a condensed printed version of the minutes (these are available in RG 267, as well as through many library collections). The Court's minutes, covering the period from 1789 to 1806, were also transcribed and published between 1961 and 1964 in the *American Journal of Legal History*.

The Supreme Court maintains both rough and engrossed dockets. Docket entries for each Court case indicate the case name, the court from which the case was appealed (if applicable), the names of the attorneys appearing for the parties, and a chronological record of the papers filed and the proceedings held. In addition, the general records include transcripts of oral arguments since 1968 and sound recordings of oral arguments since 1955 (audio versions of selected oral arguments can also be downloaded from various websites).

The general records of the Court include some case materials, including papers related to more than one case, papers and exhibits from unidentified cases, maps and charts, memorandums of pending cases, photographs, indexes, and a volume of manuscript opinions issued in 1832. The general records also include correspondence related to the Committee on Equity Practice (1911–1912), the correspondence of the Chief Justice's law clerks (1927–1938), and the private papers of Supreme Court employee Francis R. Kirkham (1931–1934).

## D. Appellate Jurisdiction Case Records

The Supreme Court's appellate case records consist of case files, indexes, opinions, copies of mandates sent to lower courts, and miscellaneous papers in undocketed cases.

Appellate case files contain transcripts of proceedings from lower courts, petitions for writs of error or certiorari, briefs, motions, orders, judgments, decrees, mandates, agreements, bonds, depositions, writs, and other papers. Appellate case files from 1792 to 1933 are arranged in one numerical sequence (case numbers 1–38,700). Since 1934, appellate case files have been arranged by term and thereunder by case number. Researchers wishing to locate particular case files can use a card index available at the National Archives that provides the title and number of each appellate case, as well as the filing and decision dates.

The Supreme Court's appellate jurisdiction records include a numerically arranged collection of manuscript opinions and revised printed appellate opinions, including both majority and dissenting opinions. The National Archives published an *Index to the Manuscript and Revised Printed Opinions of the Supreme Court of the United States in the National Archives, 1808–1873* (Washington, D.C.: The National Archives, 1965), which includes citations to both appellate and original jurisdiction cases. The Court also kept, as distinct sets of records within the Court's appellate records, duplicate mandates to lower courts, papers from undocketed appellate cases, and certiorari cards.

## E. Original Jurisdiction Case Records

Original jurisdiction case records consist of case files (1792–) and drafts of opinions (1835–1909). A fire in the U.S. Capitol in November 1898 destroyed many of the Court's original jurisdiction case files, but those that survived include bills of complaint, answers, exhibits, petitions, affidavits, subpoenas, orders, judgments, correspondence, and other related papers. Case files are arranged chronologically by term and thereunder by case number. The Court also maintained a collection of manuscript and printed opinions in cases arising under the Court's original jurisdiction. These are arranged chronologically by term and thereunder alphabetically by the name of the first party in the case.

## F. Records Relating to Ex Parte and Miscellaneous Cases

The records of the Supreme Court include three distinct sets of papers related to habeas corpus cases that were heard in individual justice's chambers, ex parte and miscellaneous case files, and papers related to applications that were denied by the Court (although it should be noted that these types of cases also appear in the Court's appellate and original jurisdiction records). These case files include petitions for writs, applications, transcripts of record from trial courts, motions, briefs, orders, returns, correspondence, opinions, writs, and other papers. Most of the petitions in these subgroups were for writs of habeas corpus, mandamus, prohibition, certiorari, or injunction, although some files also pertain to stays of execution or the disbarment of attorneys.

## G. Records of the Office of the Clerk

The records of the clerk of the Supreme Court include correspondence and other papers related to the printing of opinions, the admission of attorneys, the Court's financial operations, and the general administration of the Court.

The historical records of the Office of the Clerk include several collections of correspondence. The General Correspondence file (1791–1952) includes letters received and copies of outgoing letters relating to Court fees, the Court's docket, the filing of papers, and other administrative duties of the clerk. Other files include correspondence with the justices (1791–1926), letters related to the appointment of stenographic clerks (1888–1940), correspondence with the U.S. General Accounting Office (1949–1956), and correspondence relating to the Administrative Office of the United States Courts (1939–1942) and the Advisory Committees on Rules of Criminal and Civil Procedure (1941–1946). A "Subject File" (1800–1910) includes correspondence, memoranda, orders, subscription lists, and other papers relating to various administrative aspects of the Court.

The clerk's records include material related to the clerk's administrative duties, including oaths of office, papers related to retirements and memorial proceedings, and orders concerning rules, Court administration, and circuit allotments. Also included are miscellaneous papers and gifts received by the Court, records related to the printing and binding of Court opinions, and scrapbooks of newspaper clippings relating to Supreme Court history.

The records of the Office of the Clerk include several series of "Records Relating to Admissions to the Bar of the Court" and "Fiscal Records." The Court's bar admission records include certificates of admission to practice before the Supreme Court and state courts, Civil War-era loyalty oaths, a card index file of counselors and attorneys admitted to practice, and attorney rolls. The card index file shows the name of each attorney, the date of his or her admission, and in most cases the attorney's place of residence. Attorney rolls contain the signatures of attorneys admitted to practice, and, in some cases, attorneys' oaths or other personal information. Some entries also signify disbarment. The clerk's "Fiscal Records" include fee books, bonds, bills, lists, receipts, records of daily receipts and expenditures, and additional records related to the printing of Court opinions. These records also include correspondence with Treasury Department officials regarding the clerk's accounts.

## H. Records of the Office of the Marshal

Congress established the Office of the Marshal of the Supreme Court in 1867. Prior to that date, the marshal of the district in which the Court sat also served as the marshal of the Court. The marshal's duties have included protecting the Court and its visitors, executing the Court's orders and precepts, securing its property and facilities, disbursing funds to Court officers and employees, reporting the Court's expenses to the various executive departments charged with overseeing the administration of the federal courts, arranging for the purchase of supplies and furniture, and assisting the members of the Court with various tasks.

Most of the records of the marshal consist of correspondence and accounting records. A collection of subject files (1867–1913) includes correspondence, memorandums, newspaper clippings, and other papers related to legislation, the Court's meeting places, justices' funerals, the Columbian Exposition of 1892, presidential inaugurations, and portraits of the justices and officers of the Court. A separate file contains applications and endorsements for various positions at the Court (1867–1909), as well as for the position of register in bankruptcy (the Bankruptcy Act of 1867 authorized the Chief Justice to appoint registers in bankruptcy to serve in the U.S. district courts). In addition, the marshal's records include correspondence regarding the acquisition of books for the Court's library and for the Library of Congress, as well as a general correspondence file (1867–1940).

From 1867 to 1936, the Office of the Marshal maintained the Court's accounting records, which include receipts, statements of accounts, paperwork related to the sale of furniture, payroll receipts, cashbooks, journals, and ledgers. The marshal also corresponded regularly with officials in the Interior, Treasury, and Justice Departments concerning accounts and requisitions.

## I. Published Decisions and Other Records

The first 90 volumes of the Supreme Court's reports are called nominative reports because they are named after the person who edited and published them. In its earliest years, the Supreme Court had no official reporter, and Congress did not authorize a salaried reporter for the Court until 1817. In addition, the Court generally did not issue written opinions until the early nineteenth century. Researchers must therefore be mindful that the earliest reports of the Court's decisions contain omissions and inaccuracies and may, in fact, reflect the ideas of the reporter more than those of the justices.

The first reporter of the Supreme Court's decisions was a Pennsylvania lawyer named Alexander J. Dallas who, on his own initiative, reported the Court's decisions from 1791 to 1800—Philadelphia was the nation's capital during this period. Dallas also included a record of the Court's proceedings from the Court's 1790 terms in New York City, although there were no cases heard until 1791. Dallas's 4-volume series was originally introduced to report the decisions of the state, federal, and some colonial courts in Pennsylvania, but he included the U.S. Supreme Court's decisions for the period the Court met in Philadelphia (these appear in the last three volumes). Dallas based his reports on his personal observations of the Court's proceedings as well as notes he obtained from attorneys who attended court sessions. Dallas included a statement of the facts and issues in each reported case, a summary of the arguments presented by the attorneys, and the text of the Court's opinion as recounted or remembered.

The next reporter of the Court's decisions, William Cranch, was a judge on the Circuit Court for the District of Columbia. Cranch's nine volumes of reports, covering the Supreme Court's decisions from 1801 to 1815, are more detailed and accurate than Dallas's reports because the Court began regularly issuing written opinions during this period. Cranch noted, in the preface to his first volume, the relief he felt "by the practice which the court had adopted of reducing their opinion to writing in all cases of difficulty or importance."

Henry Wheaton became the first Court-appointed reporter in 1816. The following year Congress authorized a salary of $1,000 for the Court reporter, although Wheaton and his successors continued to publish and sell their reports privately. Wheaton's twelve volumes of reports, which covered the decisions of the Court between 1816 and 1827, contain the most detailed and scholarly annotation of any of the nominative reporters.

Wheaton's successor, Richard Peters, Jr., compiled seventeen volumes of reports between 1828 and 1843. An entrepreneur, Peters also decided to publish the reports of his predecessors, excluding any supplementary material they had added to the opinions. After a long legal battle that was ultimately decided in the Supreme Court itself, Peters was granted the legal right to publish and sell earlier Supreme Court opinions. In 1834, the Supreme Court adopted a rule requiring the justices to file their opinions with the clerk of court. This presumably made it easier for Peters to obtain and report the Court's decisions accurately, but he was dismissed from his position in 1843 because of long delays in the publication of his reports as well as for alleged inaccuracies and omissions in the volumes he produced.

Peters' last volume of reports covers the same term (1843) as the first volume compiled by his successor, Benjamin C. Howard (only Howard's 1843 volume was incorporated into the *United States Reports*). Howard reported the Court's decisions through the 1860 term in twenty-four volumes. In 1861 and 1862, Jeremiah S. Black reported two volumes of the Court's decisions. The last of the nominative reports are the twenty-three volumes compiled by John William Wallace covering the Court's twelve terms from 1863 to 1874.

For further historical and bibliographical information regarding the ninety volumes of nominative reports, see Morris L. Cohen and Sharon Hamby O'Connor's *A Guide to the Early Reports of the Supreme Court of the United States* (Littleton, Colo.: F.B. Rothman, 1995).

In 1874, Congress appropriated $25,000 for the printing of the Supreme Court's decisions. Thereafter, the Court's decisions were published in the *United States Reports*, rather than in nominative reports from which the reporter could make a profit. The previously published nominative reports were incorporated into this series as volumes 1–90. In 1889, the Court's reporter compiled and published the decisions of the Supreme Court that had been omitted by the earlier reporters. He gathered as many as he could find, although he certainly missed some of the earlier cases for which there was no written decision. These cases, in conjunction with other historical information about the Court, appear as an appendix to volume 131 of the *United States Reports*. Researchers searching for opinions by particular justices may wish to consult Linda A. Blandford and Patricia Russell Evans, comps., *Supreme Court of the United States, 1789–1980: An Index to Opinions Arranged by Justice*, 2 vols. (Millwood, N.Y.: Kraus International Publications, 1983), and *Supplement, 1980–1990* (Millwood, N.Y.: Kraus International Publications, 1994).

Chambers opinions—the opinions of individual justices on petitions and other matters presented to them in their capacity as the justices assigned to specific circuits—were not published in the *United States Reports* until 1969. Prior to that time they were selectively reported in commercially produced publications such as *The Supreme Court Reporter* (St. Paul, Minn.: West Publishing Co., 1883–) and *United States Supreme Court Reports, Lawyers' Edition* (Rochester, N.Y.: Lawyers Co-operative Publishing Company, 1882–).

In addition to their availability in RG 267, printed briefs and the transcripts of the records of lower court proceedings, dating back to the early nineteenth century, are also available at selected federal depository libraries, at the Library of Congress, and from subscription databases and other Internet sources. Researchers must note, however, that the collation, arrangement, and binding of these briefs and transcripts varies from library to library.

The editors of *The Documentary History of the Supreme Court of the United States, 1789–1800*, 7 vols. (New York: Columbia University Press, 1985–2003), compiled a wide array of primary source material from the first decade of the Supreme Court's history, covering appointments, circuit riding, the organization of the federal judiciary, and cases. The volumes reproduce various types of court records, including the Court's minutes and dockets (both rough and final), motions, orders, grand jury charges, papers related to the admission of attorneys, judges' commissions and oaths, memoranda, case papers, and opinions. The editors have also gathered supplementary materials, including diary entries, correspondence, reminiscences, draft opinions, legislation, reports of oral arguments, briefs, and notes by clerks, judges, and other court personnel. The volumes reproduce public reactions to judicial decisions, including jury responses to charges, public and private writings, and newspaper reports and editorials.

Researchers interested in locating recent Supreme Court opinions, orders, rules, calendars, and briefs will find helpful information, Internet links, and PDF versions at http://www.supremecourtus.gov/. Cases, sound recordings, and other historic materials are also available through other websites and subscription databases, including LexisNexis, Westlaw, HeinOnline, and http://www.oyez.org/.

# Chapter 4. Records of the Courts of the District of Columbia

## A. Historical Note

In an act of February 27, 1801, Congress established a circuit court for the District of Columbia. The act divided the District of Columbia into two counties—Alexandria and Washington—and authorized the court to hold sessions in each. The court was granted the same jurisdiction as the other U.S. circuit courts, as well as some of the powers of a U.S. district court. In addition to its federal jurisdiction, the circuit court exercised some of the jurisdiction of a local court, applying the law and procedures of Virginia for its Alexandria sessions and those of Maryland for its Washington sessions.

On February 13, 1801, in the Judiciary Act of 1801, Congress, as part of a sweeping reorganization of the federal judiciary, established a U.S. district court for the District of Potomac, which included the District of Columbia and adjacent portions of Maryland and Virginia. On March 8, 1802, Congress repealed the 1801 Judiciary Act, thus abolishing the district court for the District of Potomac. On April 29, 1802, Congress authorized the chief judge of the circuit court to hold two annual sessions of a district court in the District of Columbia.

In 1838, Congress created the Criminal Court of the District of Columbia, granting the court original jurisdiction in all criminal cases arising within the district, and giving appellate jurisdiction of all criminal cases to the circuit court. The circuit court ceased holding sessions in Alexandria in 1846, when that county was returned to the state of Virginia.

In 1863, Congress abolished the circuit, district, and criminal courts of the District of Columbia and established the Supreme Court of the District of Columbia. This court was granted the same authority and jurisdiction as the circuit court, and any of the four justices appointed to the Supreme Court of the District of Columbia could convene sessions of a district or criminal court. In 1936, Congress changed the name of the Supreme Court of the District of Columbia to the District Court of the United States for the District of Columbia, and in 1948 Congress renamed it the U.S. District Court for the District of Columbia.

In 1893, Congress established the Court of Appeals of the District of Columbia to exercise jurisdiction over appeals from the Supreme Court of the District of Columbia. In 1934, Congress designated the court as the U.S. Court of Appeals for the District of Columbia, and in 1948 as the U.S. Court of Appeals for the District of Columbia Circuit. The 1948 act specifically stated that the judges of the court had the same authority as the judges of the courts of appeals for the regional circuits.

At various times, Congress created courts and judgeships of local jurisdiction that affected the jurisdiction of the Article III courts in the District of Columbia. Under the act of February 27, 1801, Congress authorized the President to appoint justices of the peace and judges of an orphans' court in each county of the District. In 1909, the justices of the peace were reorganized as the Municipal Court of the District of Columbia. The circuit (and later supreme) court exercised appellate jurisdiction over the decisions of the orphans' court until 1870, when that court was abolished, and over the justices of the peace and municipal court until 1921, when Congress transferred that jurisdiction to the Court of Appeals for the District of Columbia.

In 1870, Congress created the Police Court of the District of Columbia, limiting the criminal jurisdiction of the District of Columbia Supreme Court to "capital or otherwise infamous crimes" (although the Supreme Court's criminal jurisdiction was expanded four years later so that the two courts had concurrent jurisdiction over many types of cases). Justices of the Supreme Court of the District of Columbia heard appeals from the police court until 1897, when that jurisdiction was assigned to the Court of Appeals of the District of Columbia.

The federal courts in the District of Columbia also exercised appellate jurisdiction over decisions of the commissioner of patents from 1839 to 1929, and from 1919 until 1924 the Supreme Court of the District of Columbia exercised appellate jurisdiction over decisions of the local rent commission.

The federal courts of the District of Columbia exercised a combination of federal and local jurisdiction until 1971. The District of Columbia Court Reform and Criminal Procedure Act of 1970 established two courts, the District of Columbia Superior Court and the District of Columbia Court of Appeals, to assume responsibility for local jurisdiction, similar to that exercised by state courts.

## B. Records Description

The records of the district court for the District of Potomac (1801–1802), the Circuit Court of the District of Columbia (1801–1863), the criminal court of the District of Columbia (1838–1863), the Supreme Court of the District of Columbia (1863–1936), the District Court of the United States for the District of Columbia (1936–1948), and the U.S. District Court for the District of Columbia (1948–) are included in Record Group 21 at the National Archives in Washington, D.C. (The records of the Alexandria term of the circuit court, 1801–1846, are maintained by the Library of Virginia in Richmond.) The records are organized by court and thereunder by type of case. Like other federal district and circuit courts, these records include law, appellate, criminal, bankruptcy, admiralty, habeas corpus, fugitive slave, equity, and naturalization cases, as well as other general administrative papers. District of Columbia court records also include manumission and emancipation papers, marriage licenses, lien law case files, the papers of the justices of the peace, medical licenses, probate records from the orphans' court, insolvency cases, and copyright papers. The courts' habeas records reflect the courts' partly federal and partly local jurisdiction, with many petitions relating to child custody disputes and indentured servitude. RG 21 also contains appellate records from decisions of the commissioner of patents, the orphans' courts, the police court, the justices of the peace, the municipal court, and the rent commission.

The records of the Court of Appeals for the District of Columbia, consisting of minutes, dockets, case files, briefs, transcripts of records, mandates, and attorney files, are maintained in Record Group 276 at the National Archives in Washington, D.C. The organization of these records is similar to the records of the other U.S. courts of appeals, which are described in Chapter 2, but the records also include patent case files and material relating to the exercise of the court's local jurisdiction.

Some records related to the courts of local jurisdiction in the District of Columbia are held with the records of the Government of the District of Columbia in Record Group 351 at the National Archives in Washington, D.C.

## C. Published Decisions

Circuit Judge William Cranch published the decisions of the circuit court of the District of Columbia from the court's first four decades in *Reports of Cases Civil and Criminal in the United States Circuit Court of the District of Columbia, from 1801 to 1841*, 5 volumes plus index (Boston: Little, Brown and Co., 1852–1853). The commissioner of patents published a collection of Cranch's patent decisions in *Laws of the United States Relating to Patents and the Patent Office* (Washington, D.C.: n.p., 1848). John A. Hayward and George C. Hazleton compiled decisions issued by the circuit and criminal courts between 1840 and 1863, in *Reports of Cases, Civil and Criminal, Argued and Adjudged in the Circuit Court of the District of Columbia for the County of Washington*, 2 volumes (Washington, D.C.: W. H. Lowdermilk and Co., 1892; John Byrne and Co., 1895).

The decisions of the Supreme Court of the District of Columbia from 1863 to 1893 were published in sixteen volumes by several printers in Washington, D.C., and Baltimore, in a series titled *Reports of Cases Argued and Adjudged in the Supreme Court of the District of Columbia* (the volumes covering 1873 to 1879 were titled *Reports of Cases Argued and Determined in the Supreme Court of the District of Columbia*). The decisions of the court from 1933 to 1935 were published in the short-lived *Supreme Court of the District of Columbia Reports*, 2 volumes (Washington, D.C.: National Law Book Co., 1936).

The decisions of the Court of Appeals of the District of Columbia from 1893 to 1933 were published in *Reports of Cases Adjudged in the Court of Appeals of the District of Columbia* (these reports were published by several private companies in Baltimore, Washington, D.C., and New York, until the West Publishing Co. began publishing the series in 1920). Decisions of the United States Court of Appeals for the District of Columbia from 1934 to 1939 were published in *Reports of Cases Adjudged in the United States Court of Appeals for the District of Columbia* (St. Paul, Minn.: West Publishing Co., 1935–1939). From 1939 to 1948, decisions appeared in *United States Court of Appeals for the District of Columbia, Cases Argued and Adjudged* (St. Paul, Minn.: West Publishing Co., 1940–1949), and beginning in 1948, decisions were published in *United States Court of Appeals, District of Columbia Circuit, Cases Argued and Adjudged* (St. Paul, Minn.: West Publishing Co., 1950–1955). Since 1955, decisions have been reported in *United States Court of Appeals for the District of Columbia Circuit, Cases Adjudged* (St. Paul, Minn.: West Publishing Co., 1956–).

Many of the opinions of the U.S. courts in the District of Columbia (as well as some other state and federal decisions) can be found in a weekly newspaper, *The Washington Law Reporter* (1874–1959), and its successor, *The Daily Washington Law Reporter* (1959–), as well as in *Federal Cases*, 30 volumes (St. Paul, Minn.: West Publishing Co., 1894–

1897). The West Publishing Company also publishes the opinions of the district court in the *Federal Supplement* (St. Paul, Minn.: West Publishing Co., 1932–), and of the supreme and appeals courts in the three series of the *Federal Reporter* (St. Paul, Minn.: West Publishing Co., 1880–).

Researchers interested in further information on the reported decisions of the federal courts in the District of Columbia should consult Helen Newman, "Memorials and Notes in District of Columbia Reports," *Law Library Journal* 26, 33–36 (1933), and the *District of Columbia Digest* (Washington, D.C.: Washington Law Book Co., 1936–1968; St. Paul, Minn.: West Publishing Co., 1970–).

# Chapter 5. Records of Federal Courts of Special Jurisdiction

## A. Introduction

At various times since the mid-nineteenth century, Congress has created courts of special jurisdiction to ease the caseload of the U.S. district, circuit, and appeals courts, to exercise authority formerly held by Congress or a department of the executive branch, or to review the decisions of particular federal agencies or departments. The records of these federal courts usually consist of general, case, and administrative records.

The general records of a court include minutes and dockets. Minute books, which are sometimes called journals, contain a daily account of a court's activities. Arranged chronologically, entries in the minutes indicate the actions taken by the court, including rulings on motions, the adoption of procedural rules, the admission of attorneys to the bar, and the appointment of court officers. Some courts also kept "rough" minutes, which were the volumes the clerk used to prepare the "final" or "engrossed" minutes.

Dockets contain chronological summaries of the filings and proceedings in each case. Docket entries, which are organized by case, indicate case numbers, the names of the parties and their attorneys, dates of specific filings and proceedings, and the outcome of each case. Some courts maintained a different docket for each area of the court's jurisdiction.

Case records generally consist of case files and other related materials. Case files, which are usually organized by case number, contain the original documents submitted to and issued by the court in each proceeding. These may include petitions, answers, briefs, memoranda, notices of appeal, transcripts of the record of proceedings in other courts, testimony, petitions, documents created by other government agencies, correspondence relating to the case, exhibits, orders, decrees, transcriptions of oral arguments, and the opinion of the court.

A court's administrative records include papers related to the clerk's responsibilities, the court's financial operations, and the admission of attorneys to the bar. Some courts also kept collections of miscellaneous papers, such as lists of cases, indexes to opinions, correspondence files, and other papers related to the work of the court.

## B. Court of Claims, 1855–1982

### 1. Historical Note

In 1855, Congress established a Court of Claims with jurisdiction to hear and determine monetary claims against the federal government based on congressional statutes, executive branch regulations, or contracts with the government. Previously, such claims had been submitted through petitions to Congress. At first, the new court's power was limited to investigating and reporting on claims and preparing legislative bills for payments to successful claimants, but in 1863 Congress authorized the court to issue final judgments against the United States and to consider counterclaims by the government.

The court was composed of three judges who were appointed by the President and confirmed by the Senate to serve with tenure during good behavior. Each of these judges was authorized to appoint commissioners to take depositions and issue subpoenas. The 1863 act increased the number of judges to five and permitted appeals from the Court of Claims to the Supreme Court of the United States. Congress expanded the court's jurisdiction on a number of occasions, most notably in the Tucker Act of 1887, which gave the court the authority to hear claims based on the U.S. Constitution and made the court the principal forum for all claims against the United States. The increasing volume of business before the court led Congress in 1925 to authorize the court to appoint seven commissioners, each of whom could hear evidence in specific cases and report findings of fact to the court.

The Court of Claims heard many types of cases under its grant of general jurisdiction, including cases that resulted from violations of government contracts, violations of Indian treaties, infringements on patents, unlawful imprisonments, over-assessment of taxes, cases of eminent domain, and losses of property during wartime. At various times Congress also granted the court temporary or special jurisdiction in certain types of cases.

The Court of Claims was abolished in 1982. Its judges and much of its jurisdiction were transferred to the new U.S. Court of Appeals for the Federal Circuit. In the same 1982 statute, Congress created a new "Claims Court," with jurisdiction over claims seeking money judgments from the United States. In 1992, Congress changed the name of the court to the U.S. Court of Federal Claims.

## 2. Records Description

The historical records of the Court of Claims consist of case files and supplementary case materials, dockets, journals, and registers of attorneys admitted to practice before the court (see the beginning of this chapter for a brief explanation of what is included in these types of records). Many case papers of the Court of Claims were documents submitted to the court in order to prove the validity of a claim. The court's older records have been accessioned by the National Archives and make up Record Group 123 at the National Archives in Washington, D.C. More recent records are maintained by the Court of Federal Claims, pending their accession by the National Archives.

The records of the Court of Claims are organized by type of jurisdiction, including cases referred to the court by either house of Congress (Congressional–Jurisdiction cases) or an executive department (Departmental–Jurisdiction cases), claims against the District of Columbia, claims for property taken or destroyed by Indian tribes (Indian Depredation cases), and claims for private property captured by French ships prior to 1801 (French Spoliation cases). Each jurisdictional group contains its own dockets, case files (which are sometimes divided into additional subgroups), and separate collections of related case materials.

The 1855 act establishing the Court of Claims also created the position of solicitor to represent the U.S. government in cases before the court. In 1868, this responsibility was transferred to the Office of the Attorney General, and in 1870 to the Department of Justice. The records of the Court of Claims section of the Department of Justice, contained in Record Group 205, supplement the records of the Court of Claims. RG 205, held at the National Archives in Washington, D.C., contains administrative records, correspondence, briefs, dockets, weekly reports received by the assistant attorney general, office files, transcripts of hearings and testimony, exhibits, indexes to the cases and judgments, and other miscellaneous papers. Also included in RG 205 are duplicates of many case files. Like the records in RG 123, the case papers in RG 205 are organized by type of jurisdiction. Researchers wishing to locate specific cases within RG 123 will find useful the dockets, indexes, and supplementary materials among the Department of Justice's records.

Many records related to the work of the Court of Claims are held with the records of the Treasury Department. Record Group 56, the General Records of the Department of the Treasury, includes correspondence between Treasury officials and the judges and clerks of the Court of Claims, lists of claimants, reports on claimants, registers of claims, an index to the court's dockets, copies of records that were sent from the Treasury to the court, and lists of awards made by the court. Additional correspondence related to the payment of the court's judgments can be found in the Records of the Accounting Officers of the Department of the Treasury, in RG 217. The Treasury Department records in Record Group 56 are held at the National Archives at College Park, Maryland. The records of the Treasury Department's accounting officers, in RG 217, are held at the National Archives in Washington, D.C.

Records relating to the Indian depredation cases will also be found in the Records of the Bureau of Indian Affairs (RG 75), which are located at the various regional branches of the National Archives. Textual records and maps related to Indian Tribal Claims against the United States can be found in the Records of the Government Accountability Office (RG 411).

## 3. Published Decisions

From its establishment in 1855 until 1863, the Court of Claims reported to Congress its recommendations for the disposition of claims in *Reports from the Court of Claims*, 18 vols. (Washington, D.C.: Cornelius Wendell, 1856–1857; James B. Steedman, 1858–1859; Thomas H. Ford, 1860; G.P.O., 1861–1863). In addition to the court's opinions and recommendations, these reports include copies of the petitions, briefs, and miscellaneous documents from each case.

Opinions issued by the Court of Claims between 1863 and 1982 are published, along with abstracts of the court's unwritten decisions, in *Cases Decided in the Court of Claims of the United States*, 231 vols. (Washington, D.C.: W.H. & O.H. Morrison, 1867; G.P.O., 1868–1983). Opinions issued between 1929 and 1932 and between 1960 and 1982 also appear in the *Federal Reporter, Second Series* (St. Paul, Minn.: West Publishing Co., 1924–1993), while opinions issued between 1932 and 1960 are published in the *Federal Supplement* (St. Paul, Minn.: West Publishing Co., 1932–1998).

Several digest editions of the reports of the Court of Claims have been published by private companies as well as by the Government Printing Office. The *United States Congressional Serial Set* also contains the court's opinions, lists of judgments and dismissed claims, correspondence, findings of fact, reports of the clerk of the court, and other related documents.

## C. U.S. Court of Federal Claims, 1982–

### 1. Historical Note

The U.S. Court of Federal Claims was established as the U.S. Court of Claims by the Federal Courts Improvement Act of 1982. The new court assumed the original jurisdiction of the Court of Claims, which was abolished by the act of 1982. The act of 1982 granted the U.S. Court of Claims jurisdiction to hear money claims against the federal government based on the Constitution, statutes, executive department regulations, or government contracts. Typical cases involved disputes concerning tax refunds, federal contracts, federal takings of private property, or government employees' pay. In 1992, Congress changed the name of the court to the U.S. Court of Federal Claims. The principal seat of the court is Washington, D.C., but Congress authorized the court to sit in other locations to facilitate appearances by parties and witnesses.

### 2. Records Description

Once they are accessioned, the records of the U.S. Court of Federal Claims will make up Record Group 502 at the National Archives in Washington, D.C. Some case files have been transferred to the Washington National Records Center in Suitland, Maryland, pending their accession. These files, which are boxed and undescribed, are available to researchers.

### 3. Published Decisions

Opinions issued by the U.S. Court of Federal Claims between 1982 and 1992 are published in the *United States Claims Court Reporter*, 26 vols. (St. Paul, Minn.: West Publishing Co., 1983–1993). Opinions issued by the Court since 1992 are published in the *Federal Claims Reporter* (St. Paul, Minn.: West Publishing Co., 1993–).

## D. Board of General Appraisers, 1890–1926; U.S. Customs Court, 1926–1980; U.S. Court of International Trade, 1980–

### 1. Historical Note

In order to relieve the caseload of the U.S. district and circuit courts and to regularize the procedure for settling customs disputes, Congress in 1890 established a Board of General Appraisers to decide controversies related to appraisals of imported goods and classifications of tariffs. The appraisers were nominated by the President, confirmed by the Senate, and could be removed by the President with cause. The Board operated under the direction of the Secretary of the Treasury, and it heard appeals of decisions by customs officers. Although the secretary could order appraisers to sit in any port in the country, the Board and the courts that succeeded it have had their headquarters in New York City. Appeals from the Board's decisions were reviewable by the U.S. circuit courts, and, after their establishment in 1891, the U.S. circuit courts of appeals as well. The volume of appeals grew so high that, in 1909, Congress established a Court of Customs Appeals to hear all challenges to the decisions of the Board of General Appraisers.

In 1926, Congress changed the name of the Board to the U.S. Customs Court and provided that the appraisers would be known as the chief justice and justices of the court. (Four years later the titles were changed to judge.) In several subsequent acts, Congress integrated the court into the administrative structure of the federal judiciary and established it as a court of record under Article III of the U.S. Constitution.

In 1980, Congress reorganized the U.S. Customs Court as the U.S. Court of International Trade, with nine judges appointed with tenure during good behavior. The court was granted the same judicial powers in law and equity as a U.S. district court and was authorized to issue writs, orders, injunctions, and monetary judgments. The act of 1980 also gave the Court of Customs and Patent Appeals exclusive jurisdiction over appeals from the decisions of the Court of International Trade.

The U.S. Customs Court and its predecessor, the Board of General Appraisers, were established in an era when almost all federal trade litigation related to tariffs; the court and Board served primarily to oversee the decisions of administrative agencies relating to the classification and valuation of imported goods. The jurisdiction of the U.S. Court of International Trade, by contrast, includes the adjudication of nearly all civil actions related to international trade that are brought by or against the United States.

## 2. Records Description

The National Archives has established a single record group, RG 321, for the records of the U.S. Court of International Trade and its two predecessor entities. The records of the Board of General Appraisers and the U.S. Customs Court have been transferred to the National Archives at New York City. The records of the U.S. Court of International Trade are still maintained by the court, pending their accession by the National Archives.

The records of the Board of General Appraisers include bound volumes of the Board's decisions, judgment and order books, incoming correspondence and press copies (duplicates) of letters sent, schedules of examinations, reports of meetings, indexes to the Board's decisions, a register of protests received from the Collector of Customs at New York, and miscellaneous papers.

The records of the U.S. Customs Court include the decisions of the court (these are organized by type of proceeding), card indexes to the cases, judgment and order books, indexes to the cases, and papers related to the ownership of vessels.

The records of the U.S. Circuit Court for the Southern District of New York, in Record Group 21 at the National Archives at New York City, include minutes, dockets, returns of record, and case files from suits appealing the decisions of the Board of General Appraisers, covering the period from 1890 to 1911. Later appellate records are located in the records of the U.S. Court of Customs and Patent Appeals (described below).

The unpublished decisions of the Board of General Appraisers, as well as correspondence between the Board and Treasury Department officials, are held with the General Records of the Department of the Treasury, in Record Group 56, at the National Archives at College Park, Maryland.

## 3. Published Decisions

Abstracts of the decisions of the Board of General Appraisers, along with the full text of some of the Board's written opinions, were published in *Synopsis of the Decisions of the Treasury Department on the Construction of the Tariff, Navigation, and Other Laws* (Washington, D.C.: G.P.O., 1881–1898) and *Treasury Decisions*, 101 vols. (Washington, D.C.: G.P.O., 1899–1967). *Treasury Decisions* also contains abstracts and reports of decisions issued by the U.S. Customs Court between 1926 and 1938. Later decisions of the Customs Court were reported in *United States Customs Court Reports*, 85 vols. (Washington, D.C.: G.P.O., 1939–1981) and, after 1956, in the *Federal Supplement* (St. Paul, Minn.: West Publishing Co., 1933–1998). The decisions of the U.S. Court of International Trade are reported in *United States Court of International Trade Reports* (Washington, D.C.: G.P.O., 1982–) and in the first and second series of the *Federal Supplement*.

## E. U.S. Court of Customs and Patent Appeals, 1910–1982

### 1. Historical Note

The Payne–Aldrich Tariff Act of 1909 provided for a U.S. Court of Customs Appeals to hear all appeals from the Board of General Appraisers (later known as the U.S. Customs Court) because such appeals had become a heavy burden for the U.S. circuit courts and the U.S. circuit courts of appeals, particularly those of the Second Circuit. Despite considerable opposition to the creation of a specialized appeals court, Congress approved a measure that called for a five-judge court to convene in Washington, D.C. In 1929, Congress renamed the court the U.S. Court of Customs and Patent Appeals and expanded its jurisdiction to include appeals from the Patent Office in patent and trademark cases. Such cases previously had been the jurisdiction of the Court of Appeals for the District of Columbia. The U.S. Court of Customs and Patent Appeals was abolished in 1982, when its judges and its jurisdiction were transferred to the new U.S. Court of Appeals for the Federal Circuit.

### 2. Records Description

The records of the U.S. Court of Customs and Patent Appeals were transferred to the U.S. Court of Appeals for the Federal Circuit in 1982. Some of the court's early records have since been accessioned by the National Archives and are organized as Record Group 503 at the National Archives in Washington, D.C.

 The general and administrative records of the U.S. Court of Customs and Patent Appeals include dockets, journals, rough notes (rough minutes), attorney rolls, cash books, and court calendars. The court's case records are organized by jurisdiction, with separate series of case files and briefs for customs and patent cases. Researchers can consult the introduction of this chapter for a description of a court's general, administrative, and case records. In addition to the standard types of materials found in case files, patent case files include patent drawings.

### 3. Published Decisions

The written decisions of the U.S. Court of Customs Appeals and its successor, the U.S. Court of Customs and Patent Appeals, are published in *Court of Customs Appeals Reports* (Washington, D.C.: G.P.O., 1911–1929), *Court of Customs and Patent Appeals Reports* (Washington, D.C.: G.P.O., 1930–1967), and *Cases Decided in United States Court of Customs and Patent Appeals* (Washington, D.C.: G.P.O., 1967–1983). The three series contain 69 consecutively numbered volumes, each of which includes an alphabetically arranged index of reported cases and a memorandum of cases decided without a written opinion. Volumes 17 to 59, covering the period from 1929 to 1972, are divided into two parts, with part one containing customs cases and part two containing patent cases.

## F. Commerce Court, 1910–1913

### 1. Historical Note

In 1910, Congress created the Commerce Court to hear appeals from orders of the Interstate Commerce Commission (ICC), which had been established in 1887 to regulate the nation's railroads. The court was composed of five judges appointed by the President and confirmed by the Senate to serve staggered terms of up to five years. These judges were simultaneously appointed to a U.S. circuit court of appeals upon which they could continue to serve with tenure during good behavior at the conclusion of their Commerce Court service.

The Commerce Court had jurisdiction, previously vested in the U.S. circuit courts, over cases brought to enforce, annul, set aside, or suspend the orders of the ICC, but the court's final judgments were reviewable, on appeal, by the Supreme Court of the United States. In an act of October 1913, Congress abolished the Commerce Court as of December 31, 1913. The jurisdiction of the court was assigned to the district courts, and pending cases were transferred to the district court in which the petitioning party resided.

### 2. Records Description

The records of the Commerce Court make up Record Group 172 at the National Archives in Washington, D.C. The Commerce Court's records consist of general records, case records, and miscellaneous records (see the introduction of this chapter for an explanation of the materials included in these types of records).

The general records of the Commerce Court include a docket book, engrossed and rough minutes, and a roll of attorneys admitted to practice before the court. In addition to a record of the proceedings and filings in each case, the docket gives information on Interstate Commerce Commission cases in the U.S. circuit courts prior to the creation of the Commerce Court as well as a record of the transfer of the Commerce Court's cases to the U.S. district courts in December 1913.

The court's case records include case files, a collection of records and briefs, and a separate file of stenographic transcripts of the court's oral proceedings. Records of cases pending in the Commerce Court on December 31, 1913, are part of the records of the U.S. district courts (RG 21) to which those cases were transferred.

The miscellaneous records of the Commerce Court include lists of cases pending in or filed with the court, copies of the marshal's outgoing correspondence, an index to the court's published opinions, and a bound volume of printed briefs filed in 1911 by representatives of the railroad industry and the federal government relating to the scope of the court's jurisdiction.

Researchers may also wish to consult the records of the Interstate Commerce Commission in Record Group 134, which is held at the National Archives at College Park, Maryland.

### 3. Published Decisions

The decisions of the Commerce Court were reported in the single-volume *Opinions of the United States Commerce Court* (Washington, D.C.: G.P.O., 1913). The index to *Opinions* indicates which of the decisions were also reported in volumes 188 to 209 of the *Federal Reporter* (St. Paul, Minn.: West Publishing Co., 1880–1924) as well as which cases were appealed to the Supreme Court.

## G. Emergency Court of Appeals, 1942–1961; Temporary Emergency Court of Appeals, 1971–1992

### 1. Historical Note

In 1942, Congress established the Emergency Court of Appeals as a special court with exclusive jurisdiction to decide cases arising from wartime price control measures imposed by the Emergency Price Control Act of 1942. The act authorized the Chief Justice of the United States to designate three or more U.S. district and appeals court judges to serve on the court until the Chief Justice revoked their appointment. The court exercised most of the powers of a U.S. district court, and Congress later extended its jurisdiction to cases arising under the Housing and Rent Act of 1948 and the Defense Production Act of 1950. The court heard its last case in 1961.

Congress established the Temporary Emergency Court of Appeals in December 1971 and granted it exclusive jurisdiction to hear appeals from the decisions of the U.S. district courts in cases arising under the wage and price control program of the Economic Stabilization Act of 1970. Congress authorized the Chief Justice of the United States to appoint to the temporary court three or more district and appeals court judges, each of whom was to serve on a part-time basis for an indefinite term. The court exercised the same powers as a U.S. court of appeals, and it was authorized to prescribe its own rules of practice, which it did when its three district and six appeals court judges convened for the first time in February 1972.

Although the Economic Stabilization Act expired in 1974, Congress, in the Emergency Petroleum Allocation Act of 1973, extended the operation of the Temporary Emergency Court of Appeals. The court exercised the judicial review provisions of the energy price stabilization program established by the act. The temporary court's jurisdiction was further expanded in the Energy Policy and Conservation Act of 1975 and the Emergency Natural Gas Act of 1977. In 1992, Congress abolished the Temporary Emergency Court of Appeals and transferred its jurisdiction and its pending cases to the U.S. Court of Appeals for the Federal Circuit.

## 2. Records Description

The records of the Emergency Court of Appeals and the Temporary Emergency Court of Appeals, consisting of briefs, appendices, case files, and other legal papers, are included with the records of the U.S. Courts of Appeals in Record Group 276 (see Chapter 2). The records of the Emergency Court of Appeals are held at the National Archives in Washington, D.C. The records of the Temporary Emergency Court of Appeals are available to researchers at the Washington National Records Center in Suitland, Maryland, pending transfer of the records to the National Archives.

Records related to the work of the Emergency Court of Appeals can also be found in the records of other federal agencies. Associate general counsel case files from cases tried before the Emergency Court of Appeals are held with the Records of the Office of the General Counsel in RG 188, Records of the Office of Price Administration. Transcripts of hearings before the court can be found in RG 252, Records of the Office of the Housing Expediter.

### 3. Published Decisions

The opinions issued by the Emergency Court of Appeals and the Temporary Emergency Court of Appeals of the United States were published in *Federal Reporter, Second Series* (St. Paul, Minn.: West Publishing Co., 1925–1993).

## H. Foreign Intelligence Surveillance Court, 1978–

### 1. Historical Note

In 1978, Congress established the Foreign Intelligence Surveillance Court and authorized the Chief Justice of the United States to designate seven federal district court judges to review applications for warrants related to national security investigations. The provisions for the court were part of the Foreign Intelligence Surveillance Act, which required the government, before it commenced certain kinds of intelligence gathering operations within the United States, to obtain a judicial warrant similar to that required in criminal investigations. The act required each application for a warrant to contain the Attorney General's certification that the target of the proposed surveillance was either a "foreign power" or "the agent of a foreign power" and, in the case of a U.S. citizen or resident alien, that the target may be involved in the commission of a crime. The USA Patriot Act of 2001 increased the number of judges serving on the court from seven to eleven.

The act of 1978 also established a Foreign Intelligence Surveillance Court of Review—presided over by three district or appeals court judges designated by the Chief Justice—to review, at the government's request, the decisions of the Foreign Intelligence Surveillance Court.

### 2. Records Description

The historical records of the Foreign Intelligence Surveillance Court remain classified and have not been accessioned by the National Archives. Upon accession, they will make up Record Group 477.

### 3. Published Decisions

The Foreign Intelligence Surveillance Act requires the Attorney General, in April of each year, to transmit to the Administrative Office of the United States Courts and to Congress a report setting forth the total number of applications made for orders and extensions of orders approving electronic surveillance under the act and the total number of orders and extensions either granted, modified, or denied by the Foreign Intelligence Surveillance Court during the previous year. These reports are classified and unavailable to the public.

Almost all of the orders of the Foreign Intelligence Surveillance Court are sealed. The unsealed opinions of the Foreign Intelligence Surveillance Court are published in the *Federal Supplement, Second Series* (St. Paul, Minn.: West Publishing Co., 1998–). The unsealed opinions of the Foreign Intelligence Surveillance Court of Review are published in the *Federal Reporter, Third Series* (St. Paul, Minn.: West Publishing Co., 1993–). Additional case materials for both courts, including orders, memoranda, correspondence, and other related documents, are available through Westlaw (http://www.westlaw.com).

## I. Judicial Panel on Multidistrict Litigation, 1968–

### 1. Historical Note

In 1968, Congress established the Judicial Panel on Multidistrict Litigation and granted it authority to transfer to a single district court the pretrial proceedings for civil cases involving common questions of fact. The Panel was the successor to the Coordinating Committee for Multiple Litigation for the United States District Courts, which had been established by Chief Justice Earl Warren as part of the Judicial Conference in 1962 to promote more efficient processing of the large number of antitrust cases involving electrical equipment manufacturers then pending in the federal courts. Expanding on the success of the committee's advisory role, Congress established the Panel as a national court with the authority to order transfers, conduct hearings, publish opinions, and establish its own rules of practice.

The Chief Justice of the United States appoints the members of the Judicial Panel on Multidistrict Litigation, which is composed of seven district or appeals court judges, each of whom must be from a different judicial circuit. The Panel's office is located in Washington, D.C., and it convenes in various locations around the country to facilitate the participation of parties and witnesses and to accommodate its members, who continue to serve as judges for the courts to which they were originally appointed.

### 2. Records Description

The records of the Judicial Panel on Multidistrict Litigation make up Record Group 482 at the National Archives in Washington, D.C. RG 482 includes transcripts, minutes, case files, and other records from hearings and executive sessions.

The records of the Panel's predecessor, the Coordinating Committee for Multiple Litigation (covering the year 1962 only), are included among the records of the Judicial Conference of the United States, which are part of the records of the Administrative Office of the United States Courts, in Record Group 116, at the National Archives in Washington, D.C. The collection consists of bulletins, legal complaints, correspondence, memorandums, notes, pretrial orders, and the reports of the Judicial Conference's Committee on Rules of Practice and Procedure.

## 3. Published Decisions

The opinions and orders of the Judicial Panel on Multidistrict Litigation are published in the *Federal Supplement* (St. Paul, Minn.: West Publishing Co., 1933–1998; second series, 1998–).

# Chapter 6. Records of Judicial Branch Administration

This chapter directs researchers to the historical records and publications of the judicial branch's institutions and agencies that have aided in the administration of the federal courts, served as liaisons between the judiciary and the other branches of the federal government, recommended modifications in judicial administration, and established policies for the federal courts.

## A. *Judicial Conference of the United States, 1922–*

### 1. Historical Note

The Judicial Conference of the United States serves as the governing board of the federal judiciary in administrative matters. Established in 1922 as the Conference of Senior Circuit Judges, the Conference reports to Congress on the judicial business of the United States courts and recommends possible improvements in judicial administration. In 1948, Congress changed the name of the Conference to the Judicial Conference of the United States.

The Chief Justice of the United States serves as the presiding officer of the Judicial Conference. From the Conference's inception, the chief judges of the United States courts of appeals, known until 1948 as senior circuit judges, have served as members of the Conference. In 1957, Congress expanded the membership of the Conference to include a district court judge from each circuit, and in 1986 Congress added the chief judge of the U.S. Court of International Trade.

The Judicial Conference operates through a network of committees, each of which makes policy recommendations to the larger body. Its statutory duties include making comprehensive surveys of the business in the federal courts, preparing plans for the assignment of judges to or from courts of appeals or district courts, promoting uniformity of management procedures and the expeditious conduct of business in the federal courts, reviewing and making recommendations regarding the federal rules of practice and procedure, supervising the director of the Administrative Office of the United States Courts, and reviewing the conduct and disability orders of the circuit judicial councils.

## 2. Records

The historical records of the Judicial Conference are included with the Records of the Administrative Office of the U.S. Courts in Record Group 116 at the National Archives in Washington, D.C. These records primarily relate to the Judicial Conference's committees and meetings. Records related to meetings include minutes, agendas, correspondence, reports, surveys, notes, and other related papers. Committee records include work materials generated by the committees as well as the committees' final reports. Committee records contain minutes of committee meetings, agendas, transcripts of testimony, correspondence, memoranda, surveys, orders for supplies, and other miscellaneous papers relating to committee activities.

The records of the General Services Administration, in Record Group 269 at the National Archives at College Park, Maryland, include two boxes of papers related to the Committee on Judicial Review of the President's Conference on Administrative Procedures (1953–1954), which was called by President Eisenhower at the request of the Chief Justice of the United States as chairman of the Judicial Conference. The files in RG 269 include the published reports of the Conference on Administrative Procedures, lists of consultants, proposed legislation, recommendations to the Judicial Conference, correspondence, Conference bulletins, reports adopted by the Judicial Conference, copies of law review articles on judicial review, and other miscellaneous papers.

## 3. Publications

*The Report of the Proceedings of the Judicial Conference of the United States*, which has been published under various titles since 1924, is the official record of the Conference. The Chief Justice of the United States submits the report to Congress shortly after each Conference meeting, and the report is distributed widely throughout the judicial and executive branches of the government. A memorandum of the Conference's first two meetings, convened on December 28, 1922, and September 26, 1923, was published in "The Federal Judicial Council," *Texas Law Review* 2 (1924): 458–63. Reports submitted between 1924 and 1939, and in 1942 and 1943, were published as part of *The Annual Report of the Attorney General of the United States* (Washington, D.C.: G.P.O., 1924–1939, 1942–1943); the Conference's 1944 report was never published. Reports issued in 1940 and 1941, and from 1945 to 2004, were published in single volumes with the *Annual Report of the Director of the*

*Administrative Office of the United States Courts* (Washington D.C.: G.P.O., 1940–1941, 1945–1990; Administrative Office of the United States Courts, 1991–2004). In 2005, the Administrative Office of the United States Courts began printing a semiannual *Report of the Proceedings of the Judicial Conference of the United States*.

Conference reports contain information about the state of the dockets in the federal courts, descriptions of Conference meetings and lists of judges in attendance; the reports also include the recommendations and resolutions of the Conference and the Attorney General regarding proposed legislation, the need for additional judgeships, the salaries of court officers and employees, and other matters affecting the business of the federal judiciary.

## B. *Administrative Office of the United States Courts, 1939–*

### 1. Historical Note

In 1939, Congress established the Administrative Office of the United States Courts as the first agency dedicated solely to the administration of the federal judiciary. Unlike the executive branch departments that had previously provided centralized administrative support for the federal courts (see Part III), the Administrative Office operated under the direction of the Conference of Senior Circuit Judges (later renamed the Judicial Conference). The Administrative Office assumed most of the judiciary-related duties formerly exercised by the Department of Justice, including the preparation of budget requests, the disbursal of appropriated funds, procurement, and the compilation of statistics related to court business. Pursuant to the originating statute, the Supreme Court selected the director of the Administrative Office until 1990; in 1990 Congress authorized the Chief Justice to appoint the director and deputy director, with the concurrence of the Judicial Conference. The agency continues to provide support for the day-to-day operation of the federal courts and for the Judicial Conference.

### 2. Records

The records of the Administrative Office of the United States Courts make up Record Group 116 at the National Archives in Washington, D.C. RG 116 includes general administrative records as well as separate collections that are organized by office (director, assistant director, or deputy director), division, or committee. Within each of these groups are collections of correspondence, subject files, reports, publications, surveys, memoranda, bulletins, circulars, speeches, published papers, and statistics. Many of the records within RG 116 relate to proposed legislation, the budget of the judiciary, general court rules and administration, or the particular work of each division or committee.

## 3. Publications

*The Annual Report of the Director of the Administrative Office of the United States Courts* (Washington D.C.: G.P.O., 1940–1941, 1945–1990; Administrative Office of the United States Courts, 1991–) contains summaries of new and proposed legislation affecting the courts, as well as a variety of statistical information related to the caseload, budget, and personnel of the federal judiciary. From 1940 until 2004, the director's annual report was published in the same volume as the *Report of the Proceedings of the Judicial Conference of the United States*.

Over time, the director's report came to be divided into two component parts, one focusing on the business of the courts and the other on the activities of the Administrative Office. In addition to being available with the *Proceedings of the Judicial Conference* until 2004, these parts have been published as two separate reports, entitled *Judicial Business of the United States Courts* (published since 1999) and *Activities of the Administrative Office of the United States Courts* (published since 1990). Since 2005, *Judicial Business* and *Activities* have only been available as separate publications.

The Administrative Office publishes two periodicals, *The Third Branch: A Bulletin of the Federal Courts* (1968–) and *Federal Probation: A Journal of Correctional Philosophy and Practice* (1937–), as well as a variety of statistical reports, monographs, manuals, and codes of conduct for judges and judicial branch employees. (Initially *The Third Branch* was published by the Federal Judicial Center. From 1970 to 1989 the Federal Judicial Center and Administrative Office jointly published it, and thereafter it was published exclusively by the Administrative Office.) Recent Administrative Office publications can be viewed or downloaded from the official website of the federal courts: http://www.uscourts.gov/.

## C. Federal Judicial Center, 1967–

### 1. Historical Note

In 1967, Congress established the Federal Judicial Center to carry out research related to the administration of justice and court management, to provide education and training for federal judges and court personnel, and to assist and advise the Judicial Conference on matters related to the administration and management of the courts. More recent legislation has expanded the Center's mandate to include, among other things, programs related to the history of the federal judiciary and to international judicial affairs. The Federal Judicial Center is governed by its Board, consisting of the Chief Justice, who serves as chair, the director of the Administrative Office, and seven judges appointed by the Judicial Conference. The Board selects the Center's director and deputy director.

## 2. Records

The records of the Federal Judicial Center make up Record Group 516 at the National Archives in Washington, D.C. These records include the office files of the Center's directors, subject files related to the Center's research and programs, and copies of Center publications.

The office files of the Center's directors contain correspondence, speeches, miscellaneous papers, and reports relating to the work and organization of the federal judiciary. The Center's collection of subject files documents the Center's research projects, many of which were assigned to the agency by the Judicial Conference. Subject files include correspondence, the working papers of the various divisions and groups within the agency, drafts of publications, and copies of speeches given by the Center's directors and deputy directors. RG 516 also includes Federal Judicial Center publications.

## 3. Publications

The Federal Judicial Center's *Annual Report* (Washington, D.C.: G.P.O., 1968–1969, n.p., 1970; Federal Judicial Center, 1971–) describes the various education and research projects undertaken by the Center. In addition, it includes information about the history and organization of the agency, details about the Center's budget, and lists and summaries of its various publications.

The numerous reports, manuals, pamphlets, brochures, and other materials published by the Federal Judicial Center since 1968 are listed and described in the Center's online publications catalogue. Many of these publications can be viewed or downloaded from the Center's website: http://www.fjc.gov/. Reports of the proceedings of the Center's seminars for newly appointed federal judges in the 1960s and 1970s were published in *Federal Rules Decisions* (St. Paul, Minn.: West Publishing Co., 1940–).

## D. Circuit Judicial Councils, 1939–

### 1. Historical Note

In 1939, Congress established circuit judicial councils to oversee the administration of the federal courts within each respective circuit. Congress mandated that these councils convene at least twice each year to review the caseload reports of the Administrative Office of the U.S. Courts and to issue instructions to the district judges within the circuit to expedite the courts' business. In 1980, Congress broadened the councils' mandate to include making "all necessary and appropriate orders for the effective and expeditious administration of justice within its circuit." The councils' duties include reviewing and revising local rules of practice to ensure their consistency with national rules, making temporary assignments for district and circuit judges, and reviewing complaints of judicial misconduct.

Under the 1939 statute, only the court of appeals judges in each circuit sat on a circuit judicial council. Since 1990, the councils have included an equal number of district and circuit judges, as well as the chief circuit judge, who presides over the council's meetings.

In 1971, Congress authorized each circuit judicial council to appoint a circuit executive to "exercise such administrative powers and perform such duties as may be delegated" by the council. The circuit executive's responsibilities include the administration of "all nonjudicial activities" of the circuit's court of appeals as well as oversight of many other aspects of the court's administration.

### 2. Records

The meeting files of the circuit judicial councils and the records of the circuit executives are included with the Records of the U.S. Courts of Appeals (RG 276) at the various regional branches of the National Archives. The administrative records of the circuit executives include materials related to judicial conferences, reports, correspondence, and other miscellaneous papers. To date, few of these records have been accessioned by the National Archives.

Council orders relating to complaints of judicial misconduct and disability are available for public research either at the circuit clerk's office or on the website of the courts of appeals. Selected reports of the proceedings of the circuit councils are also published in *Federal Rules Decisions* (St. Paul, Minn.: West Publishing Co., 1940–).

## E. Circuit Judicial Conferences, 1939–

### 1. Historical Note

In 1939, Congress mandated the holding of circuit judicial conferences to provide judges and lawyers a forum "for the purpose of considering the state of the business of the courts and advising ways and means of improving the administration of justice within the circuit." In 1990, Congress gave the chief judge of each circuit the option to hold conferences biennially rather than annually, and in 1996 Congress made the holding of these conferences optional. Most circuits continue to convene the conferences on an annual basis.

### 2. Records

Circuit judicial conferences generate few records that are retained at the National Archives. Conference proceedings are generally documented in the programs and agendas that are distributed to attendees. Other conference records include responses to invitations, newspaper clippings, reports of the chief judges of the district courts, transcripts of conference meetings, and other miscellaneous conference materials. Few of these records have been accessioned by the National Archives. Those that have been are included with the Records of the U.S. Courts of Appeals (RG 276) at the regional branches of the National Archives. The Records of the Administrative Office of the U.S. Courts (RG 116) also include conference committee reports, minutes, agendas, studies, memorandums, copies of speeches, and correspondence between the director of the Administrative Office and the chief judges of the courts of appeals regarding the agendas of the circuit conferences.

## F. United States Sentencing Commission, 1984–

### 1. Historical Note

Congress established the United States Sentencing Commission in 1984 as an independent commission within the judicial branch responsible for establishing sentencing policies and practices for the federal courts. The Sentencing Commission establishes guidelines that prescribe a range of sentences for federal judges to use in criminal cases. The guidelines, as amended and approved by Congress from time to time, have been in effect since 1987. The Commission conducts research on crime and sentencing issues, provides public information on these issues, and advises Congress and the executive branch on crime policy. The Commission submits proposed amendments to the guidelines to Congress and provides reports to the Judicial Conference and members of the executive branch on matters related to crime policy and sentencing.

The seven voting members of the Commission—at least three of whom must be federal judges and no more than four of whom can be from the same political party—are appointed by the President to six-year terms. The Attorney General, or a designee thereof, serves as a non-voting member, as does the chair of the U.S. Parole Commission.

## 2. Records

The National Archives has designated Record Group 539 as the Records of the United States Sentencing Commission, but to date no records have been accessioned. Certain records are available for public research through the Sentencing Commission's Office of Legislative and Public Affairs, in Washington, D.C. These materials include agendas, transcripts of public hearings, minutes of public meetings, public comments on proposed amendments to the sentencing guidelines, data and reports, and written public testimony. Minutes from public meetings, witnesses' written statements, and transcripts of testimony from public hearings are also available through the Commission's website (http://www.ussc.gov/).

Some of the Sentencing Commission's data on sentencing practices (excluding case and defendant identifiers) are available to researchers through the University of Michigan's Inter-University Consortium for Political and Social Research and can be accessed from the Consortium's website (http://www.icpsr.umich.edu/). Commission data that have been incorporated into the datasets of the Federal Justice Statistics Resource Center, which is sponsored by the Bureau of Justice Statistics and developed by the Urban Institute, are available at http://fjsrc.urban.org/.

## 3. Publications

Proposed amendments to the Sentencing Guidelines are published, with a request for public comment, in the *Federal Register* (Washington, D.C.: G.P.O., 1936–). The Commission's other publications include its *Annual Report* (Washington, D.C.: G.P.O., 1987–); the *Guidelines Manual* (Washington, D.C.: G.P.O., 1987–), which contains the Commission's guidelines, commentary, and policy statements; the *Sourcebook of Federal Sentencing Statistics* (Washington, D.C.: G.P.O., 1996–), which had previously appeared as the descriptive statistics portion of the *Annual*

*Report*; and the Commission's newsletter, *GuideLines* (Washington, D.C.: U.S. Sentencing Commission, 1995–). The Sentencing Commission also publishes various reports for Congress on specific topics relating to crime and sentencing. Most of the Commission's reports and publications, as well as its Resource Guide, can be viewed on the Commission's website (http://www.ussc.gov/).

# Chapter 7. Records of Other Courts

The records of several pre-federal and temporary courts are maintained with the records of the federal courts at the various branches of the National Archives.

The records of the Supreme Court of the United States, in Record Group 267 at the National Archives in Washington, D.C., include the records of the pre-federal Court of Appeals in Cases of Capture. The Continental Congress established the Court of Appeals in 1780 to hear appeals in prize cases from the courts of the thirteen colonies (from 1776 until the establishment of the court in 1780, the Continental Congress considered these appeals). The records of the court, which date from 1772 to 1789, include case files and other case-related papers, minutes, resolutions, lists of cases, and records from the Continental Congress. In 1792, Congress transferred the records of the Court of Appeals in Cases of Capture to the clerk of the Supreme Court.

The records of the U.S. district and circuit courts in RG 21 at the regional branches of the National Archives also include several collections of pre-federal and provisional court records. The records of the Vice Admiralty Court of the Province of New York (1685–1838) and of the Court of Admiralty of the State of New York (1784–1788) (which include admiralty and piracy case papers, minutes, lists, and miscellaneous records), have been accessioned with the records of the Southern District of New York at the National Archives at New York City. Similar admiralty records for the province and state of South Carolina (1716–1789) are included with the records of the District of South Carolina at the National Archives at Atlanta. The records of the Eastern District of Louisiana, at the National Archives at Fort Worth, include the records of the U.S. Provisional Court for the state of Louisiana, which was established by executive order in 1862. These records, which cover the years 1863 to 1865, include minutes, dockets, case files, indexes to judgments, and records concerning land condemnation. The records of the District Court for the District of Puerto Rico, at the National Archives at New York City, include the records of the U.S. Provisional Court of Puerto Rico (1899–1900), which include a criminal docket and indexes to criminal cases.

States that joined the Confederacy during the Civil War continued to create judicial records. In some instances court personnel used the same minute or docket books as the preceding U.S. district or circuit court. In other instances they began keeping new books. In addition to the standard types of court records, including law, equity, criminal, habeas, admiralty, and clerks' records, the most prevalent type of case records from the Confederate courts are case files that resulted from the Sequestration Act, adopted by the Confederate Congress in 1861. The records of the Confederate judiciary are generally maintained as a distinct unit within the records of a federal judicial district within RG 21, except in instances when the Confederate court used the same books as the previous or subsequent U.S. court. Additional Confederate court records are maintained in two other groups: Record Group 365, the Treasury Department Collection of Confederate Records, held at the National Archives in Washington, D.C., and at College Park, Maryland; and Record Group 109, the War Department Collection of Confederate Records, held at the National Archives in Washington, D.C.

Many records of territorial courts have also been accessioned with Record Group 21. Throughout the history of the federal government, Congress has established courts for the organized territories of the United States, and these courts have generally exercised a combination of federal and local jurisdiction. The records created by the territorial courts were typically transferred to the federal district court that was established when the territory became a state and are now generally maintained as a distinct series of records within the records of the subsequent district court. Territorial records are organized similarly to the records of the U.S. district courts, except that the territorial records contain additional material of a local nature. Some territorial court records remain in the custody of state archives and private libraries.

Many of the executive branch records described in Part III of this guide include materials related to territorial courts. The National Archives' collection of "Territorial Papers" in Record Group 59 (General Records of the Department of State), for example, contains material relating to the creation and maintenance of various courts in the federal territories. Correspondence in the records of the Attorney General and Department of Justice in Record Group 60 also contains information about the administration of justice in the territories.

Territorial court decisions were sporadically reported and published in individual territorial court reporters and in the following regional reporters: the *North Western Reporter* (St. Paul, Minn.: West Publishing Co., 1879–), the *Pacific Reporter* (St. Paul, Minn.: West Publishing Co., 1884–), and the *South Western Reporter* (St. Paul, Minn.: West Publishing Co., 1887–). Researchers interested in the archival records and published opinions of territorial courts should also consult Michael Chiorazzi and Marguerite Most, eds., *Prestatehood Legal Materials: A Fifty-State Research Guide, Including New York City and the District of Columbia*, 2 vols. (New York: The Haworth Press, 2005), and David W. Parker, ed., *Calendar of Papers in Washington Archives Relating to the Territories of the United States (to 1873)* (Washington, D.C.: Carnegie Institution of Washington, 1911).

The National Archives also holds the records of federal courts that are outside of the judiciary. These courts are served by judges who do not have the Article III protections of service during good behavior or exemption from salary reductions, and the administration of these courts is not governed by the policies of the Judicial Conference of the United States. Most of the federal courts outside the judiciary were established by the Congress to carry out a legislative power, such as the determination of taxes or the governance of the armed forces.

The records of the U.S. Tax Court, which was established by Congress in 1969 as a successor to the Tax Court and the Board of Tax Appeals, are held in Record Group 308 at the National Archives in Washington, D.C., and at College Park, Maryland. The records of the U.S. Court of Appeals for the Armed Forces are returned to the branch of the military from which the case was appealed. Once accessioned, the records of the U.S. Court of Appeals for Veterans Claims, which was established in 1988, will make up Record Group 521 at the National Archives. The records of the Merit Systems Protection Board, which was established in 1978 to hear appeals of personnel actions in the federal civil service, are held at the National Archives at College Park, Maryland, in RG 479, with related records in the Records of the Office of Personnel Management (RG 478) and the Records of the U.S. Civil Service Commission (RG 146). Case files and correspondence related to the United States Court for China (1906–1943) can also be found in Record Group 118, Records of the U.S. Attorneys, and Record Group 527, Records of the United States Marshals Service.

# Part II. Congressional Records Related to the Judiciary

## Historical Note

Article III of the U.S. Constitution grants Congress authority to establish inferior federal courts and to define much of those courts' jurisdiction. Since 1789, Congress has created various types of federal courts, established judicial districts and circuits and redrawn their boundaries, defined federal jurisdiction within the limits set by the Constitution, determined judicial salaries, appropriated the annual budget for the judiciary, and established administrative support agencies for the courts. The Constitution also grants the House of Representatives and the Senate a central role in the impeachment of federal judges, and the Senate has the unique power to confirm or reject judicial nominees put forward by the President.

The records of both houses of the U.S. Congress provide insight into the work of the federal judiciary and the relationship between Congress and the courts. Congress received numerous letters, petitions, memorials, and resolutions from judges, litigants, elected officials, court officers, attorneys, and other persons interested in the organization and jurisdiction of the courts as well as other matters of importance to the judiciary, the legal profession, and the general public. These congressional records help illuminate how the public has viewed the federal judiciary throughout United States history. These records also document various calls for reorganization of the judicial system. Records related to bills and legislation reveal the processes by which changes in the judicial system have been proposed or enacted. The impeachment records of Congress document the legislative branch's important disciplinary role over the judicial branch as part of the federal government's system of checks and balances. The Senate's records of executive proceedings reveal its responsibility to advise and consent to presidential nominees to the federal bench and other court offices.

# Chapter 8. Records of the U.S. Congress

The archival records of the U.S. Congress are maintained in several record groups at the National Archives in Washington, D.C. The records of the U.S. Senate are maintained in Record Group 46; the records of the U.S. House of Representatives are in Record Group 233. Within each record group, the records are arranged chronologically by Congress, and thereunder in series according to the type of record, including records of legislative proceedings (which include committee records), records of impeachment proceedings, and, for the Senate, records of executive proceedings. Since the mid-1960s, Senate committee records have been accessioned by the National Archives in collections that cover multiple Congresses. These more recent records are therefore organized by committee rather than by Congress.

General Senate records are closed to public research for twenty years; general House of Representatives records are closed to researchers for thirty years. The investigative and impeachment records of both houses are closed for fifty years. The staff of the Center for Legislative Archives at the National Archives is available to assist researchers in the use of congressional records. Researchers can contact the Center for Legislative Archives by phone at 202-357-5350 or by email at legislative.archives@nara.gov.

Many records of Congress have been published by the federal government, scholarly presses, and private companies. Published records of the Senate and House of Representatives include laws, records of debates, hearings, journals, official documents, committee reports, committee prints, and documentary editions of congressional materials. A rich collection of congressional records is also available on the Internet.

## A. Records of Legislative Proceedings: Introduction

Both the Senate and the House of Representatives maintain series of archival records related to their legislative proceedings. These series are composed of several subseries, including collections of minutes and journals, bills and resolutions, committee papers and reports, bill files or accompanying papers, petitions and memorials, presidential messages, and miscellaneous records. Minutes and journals, bills and resolutions, presidential messages, and miscellaneous records document the work of the whole House and Senate. The other subseries—committee papers and reports, petitions and memorials, and bill files or accompanying papers—document the work of the various committees of the House and Senate.

The records of legislative proceedings described in this chapter include documents received by and created by both houses of the U.S. Congress in the process of considering legislation, conducting hearings, and carrying out Congress's other legislative functions. These records are organized into subseries, as described above. To simplify the description of these records, however, this guide describes the records of legislative proceedings in two sections: (1) General Records of the Senate and House of Representatives and (2) Records of Congressional Committees.

## B. General Records of the Senate and House of Representatives

### 1. Minutes and Journals

Article I, Section 5 of the U.S. Constitution requires each house of the U.S. Congress to "keep a journal of its proceedings, and from time to time publish the same, excepting such parts as may in their judgment require secrecy; and the yeas and nays of the members of either House, on any question, shall, at the desire of one-fifth of those present, be entered in the journal." The minutes of the House and Senate, in Record Groups 233 and 46, respectively, provide a record of the daily proceedings in each house of Congress, including the votes and amendments to bills related to the federal judiciary. Generally, each house kept a different minute book for each session of Congress. In many early sessions, the houses kept a "rough" legislative journal in addition to a transcribed and corrected copy. In some instances, the Senate also kept a separate journal of the proceedings in impeachment cases.

The minutes of the House and Senate are transcribed and published as the *Journal of the House of Representatives* and the *Journal of the Senate*, providing a printed, indexed, and easily accessible account of the business considered by each house and the votes or other actions that were taken on those matters. The published *Journals* are widely available in libraries throughout the nation. Many of the early *Journals* have been digitized and placed online (see Internet Resources below).

Researchers can track the progress of bills in each house of Congress through the houses' respective *Journals*. Beginning with the Eighteenth Congress (1823–1825), the House *Journal* included a table indicating when each House and Senate bill was introduced, when the bill was amended and passed by each house of Congress, and when it was approved by the President. Beginning with the second session of the Twenty-Fourth Congress (1836–1837), the Senate *Journal* included a similar "Table of Bills."

## 2. Bills and Resolutions

Both the House of Representatives and the Senate have maintained files of bills and resolutions that originated in their own chamber as well as files of bills that were first introduced in the other house. Within each of these series, bills and resolutions are arranged by session and thereunder by number. Researchers can follow amendments to bills through annotated copies in these files. Researchers can also access published versions of bills and resolutions in their various amended forms at the National Archives, the Library of Congress, and federal depository libraries.

## 3. Miscellaneous Records

Both houses of Congress maintained other series of records that have limited amounts of information related to the judiciary. Messages received from the executive branch appear under various headings, including "Messages, Reports and Communications which were Tabled," "President's Messages," and other titles. Executive branch messages often include reports from the heads of the executive branch departments and messages from the President (related to subjects other than presidential nominations). Executive branch reports, which are usually published and available in the *United States Congressional Serial Set* (see section L, below), can include information related to judicial appropriations and finances, court meeting places, caseload statistics, and other subjects (see the sections on the published records of the executive branch departments in Part III).

The House of Representatives also kept reports from the Court of Claims, which sent Congress brief statements of recently adjudicated cases. Many of these papers are also available in the *Serial Set*.

## C. *Records of Congressional Committees*

The records of the committees of the House and Senate from 1789 until the early 1960s are organized into subseries of committee reports and papers, petitions and memorials, and bill files or accompanying papers that document the work of each committee in each house of Congress.

The holdings for each of these subseries are often inconsistent or duplicative, so a researcher interested in all documents of one category, such as petitions, will need to examine all of the subseries for that committee.

Since the early 1960s, the records of congressional committees and subcommittees have been organized in aggregate files for individual committees. The House committees continue to organize records by Congress for deposit at the National Archives. The Senate committees, however, send records to the National Archives in larger groups that may include committee records that span several Congresses. The National Archives maintains these records in the way they were arranged at the time of the accession.

Researchers interested in federal judicial history will likely find most of the archival materials they need among the records of the House and Senate committees on the judiciary. The House of Representatives established a standing Committee on the Judiciary in 1813. Since then, the committee has reported to the full House of Representatives on most legislation regarding the structure of the federal courts and the service of judges.

In 1816, the Senate established its Committee on the Judiciary as one of its original standing committees. Since then, the committee has been responsible for reporting to the full Senate on legislation regarding the structure, administration, jurisdiction, and proceedings of the federal courts, as well as on legislation related to the service of federal judges. Throughout the nineteenth century, the Senate Committee on the Judiciary frequently considered petitions and other appeals for additional judgeships, new district courts, changes in the meeting places of federal courts, and increases in judicial salaries. The committee also played a central role in drafting the legislation establishing independent administrative agencies for the judiciary in the twentieth century. The Senate Judiciary Committee has been responsible for the initial consideration of the nominations of federal judges and justices of the Supreme Court.

## 1. Committee Reports and Papers

The reports and papers of the House and Senate committees are arranged by Congress and then by committee. Committee reports explain the committee's majority (and sometimes minority) views on proposed legislation, petitions, memorials, and other matters referred to the committee. Committee papers include documents submitted to the committees by various persons, organizations, or government entities. Initially the committees of the House and Senate filed their reports and papers as a single series. Beginning with the Thirtieth Congress (1847–1849), Senate committees maintained committee papers and reports separately; the committees of the House of Representatives adopted that filing system during the Thirty-Seventh Congress (1861–1863).

The House and Senate judiciary committees' papers include petitions and memorials, hearings, committee prints, and correspondence related to the work and actions of the committee. (The committee papers may include copies of reports that are normally organized separately.) The judiciary committees often received correspondence from the Secretary of the Interior, the Attorney General, and other executive department officials related to the federal judiciary. Attorneys and other citizens also frequently corresponded with the committees regarding the organization and jurisdiction of the courts in their district or circuit, and court officers often asked the committees for increases in their salaries or the fees that they could charge for judicial services. Some correspondence included enclosures related to the work of the courts and court officers, such as statements of the fees and expenses of clerks, marshals, and U.S. attorneys. The committee papers of the Senate Judiciary Committee also include two volumes of press copies (duplicates) of letters sent (1885–1893).

The committee papers of the House and Senate judiciary committees also include minute and docket books that document the work of the committees. The House Judiciary Committee's docket books (extant from 1827 to 1913) list the bills and documents that were referred to the committee and the committee's actions taken on those matters. The House Judiciary Committee's minute books (1857–) detail the meetings and activities of the committee (including activities related to impeachments) and, in some cases, also its subcommittees. The Senate Judiciary Committee has maintained minutes of committee meetings (since 1865, with gaps), legislative dockets (1845–1896), executive dockets (1865–1941), published legislative calendars (1895–1934), and other miscellaneous registers.

Since 1903, when the House Judiciary Committee initiated distinct series of committee papers and bill files (described below), committee papers have served as a "catchall series" that include assorted records that do not fit into the bill files or the petitions and memorials files.

Since the mid-twentieth century, the standing and select subcommittees of the House and Senate judiciary committees have performed much of the legislative and investigative work of the judiciary committees. The papers of these subcommittees include correspondence, legislative case files, meeting minutes, hearing transcripts, reports and related papers, newspaper clippings files, committee prints, personnel and financial records, legal reference files, subject files, and other assorted records. Most of the Senate Judiciary Committee's subcommittee records date from 1947. Most of the House Judiciary Committee's subcommittee records date from the late 1940s and early 1950s. The scope, content and arrangement of House and Senate subcommittee records depends largely upon the workload and filing practices of each subcommittee.

## 2. Petitions and Memorials

Petitions and memorials referred to the House and Senate judiciary committees often concerned proposed legislation related to the courts, the organization and jurisdiction of the judiciary, judicial salaries and fees, court meeting places, federal bankruptcy legislation, the creation of additional judgeships, and the enforcement of federal laws. Other petitions and memorials were submitted in support of or opposition to pending legislation, requests for the repeal of laws, the impeachment of federal judges, and other various proposals related to the judiciary. Petitioners and memorialists included state legislatures, attorneys, judges, court officers, litigants in cases, bankrupts, state legislators, governors, members of local bars, officials of the executive branch departments, and other interested persons.

The petitions and memorials files in Record Groups 46 and 233 are arranged by Congress and thereunder by committee. Prior to the establishment of the Senate Committee on the Judiciary in 1816, petitions related to the judiciary were considered by temporary select committees that the Senate established to handle specific matters or perform certain functions. These earliest petitions and memorials are arranged by subject. Petitions to the House Committee on the Judiciary date from the Fifteenth Congress (1817–1819). Prior to the establishment of the House Judiciary Committee, judiciary-related petitions and memorials were often referred to the Committee of the Whole House or to a select committee that was formed to handle specific legislative matters.

Selected petitions and memorials received by Congress were published in the *Serial Set*, described below. Resolutions received from state legislatures were usually published in that state's statute books. Brief summaries of petitions and memorials that were introduced in either chamber are included in the House or Senate *Journal*, as well as in the published record of the debates of Congress.

### 3. Bill Files or Accompanying Papers

Since 1903, the committees of the House of Representatives have maintained "bill files," which are also known as "papers accompanying specific bills and resolutions." The bill files for each Congress are organized by committee and are thereunder arranged either numerically by bill number or alphabetically by name. The House Judiciary Committee's bill files often related to the organization and jurisdiction of the courts, the creation of additional judgeships, and other judiciary-related matters. Bill files contain copies of bills (often showing the amendments that were made to them), committee reports, published hearings, transcripts of unpublished hearings, petitions and memorials, correspondence, analyses by committee staff, memorandums, and other miscellaneous materials. Since 1947, House Judiciary Committee bill files have been arranged by Congress and thereunder into three topical series: "public bills and resolutions," "claims," and "immigration and naturalization legislation."

The Senate Judiciary Committee has maintained similar "legislative case files," commonly known as "accompanying papers," since 1947. From 1955 to 1966, the Senate Judiciary Committee also maintained similar files for legislative proposals that were never introduced to the full Senate. The Senate Judiciary Committee's post-1946 legislative case files supersede the earlier series of committee papers.

## D. *Records of Other Senate Committees*

The Legislative Reorganization Act of 1946 invested the Senate Committee on the Judiciary with jurisdiction that had previously been exercised by other standing committees, including the Committee on Patents (1837–1946) and the Committee on Immigration (1889–1946). The records of other committees, including the Committee on the Revision of the Laws (1869–1928), and the select and standing committees on woman suffrage (1881–1921), also contain materials related to the work of the federal courts.

The records of other Senate standing and select committees include materials that may be of interest to researchers in the history of the federal judiciary. Researchers may find records related to appropriations and finances in the records of the Committee on Finance (1816–) and the Committee on Appropriations (1867–). Researchers interested in the history of courthouses may wish to examine the records of the Committee on Public Buildings and Grounds (1838–1946) and its successors, the Committee on Public Works (1947–1977) and the Committee on the Environment and Public Works (1977–). The records of the Committee on Public Buildings and Grounds include "legislative case files" related to public buildings outside of Washington, D.C. Materials related to the Court of Claims and to claims against the United States are held with the records of the Committee on Claims (1816–1946). The Senate records of the Seventy-Sixth Congress (1939–1941) also include the papers of the Special Committee on the Reorganization of the Courts, which include meeting and hearing transcripts, minutes, charts related to court workload statistics, and miscellaneous papers.

## E. Records of Other House of Representatives Committees

In 1946, the Legislative Reorganization Act merged the jurisdiction of several House standing committees into the Committee on the Judiciary. The records of these committees may be of interest to researchers in federal judiciary history. The committees include the Committee on Claims (1794–1946), the Committee on Patents (1837–1946), the Committee on Immigration and Naturalization (1893–1946), the Committee on Revisal and Unfinished Business (1795–1868), and its successor, the Committee on Revision of Laws (1868–1946). Other standing and select committees handled matters related to the judiciary, including the Select Committee on Freedmen's Affairs (1866–1875), the Committee on Alcoholic Liquor Traffic (1893–1927), and the Committee on Woman Suffrage (1917–1927).

The records of other House standing and select committees may also have materials of interest to researchers in federal judiciary history. Researchers may find records related to appropriations and finances in the records of the Committee on Ways and Means (1795–) and the Appropriations Committee (1865–). Researchers interested in the history of courthouses may wish to examine the records of the Select Committee on Public Buildings (1819–1837) and its successors, the Committee on Public Buildings and Grounds (1837–1946), the Committee on Public Works (1946–1974), the Committee on Public Works and Transportation (1974–1994), and the Committee on Transportation and Infrastructure (1995–).

## F. Records of Joint Congressional Committees

The records of the joint committees of Congress may also have materials of interest to researchers in judicial history. The joint committees that were established during Reconstruction frequently dealt with matters of law enforcement in the United States, particularly in the Southern states. The Joint Committee on the Revision of the Laws (1907–1910) includes records related to the revision and codification of federal statutes The National Archives has placed the records of the joint congressional committees into their own record group, RG 128, at the National Archives in Washington, D.C. Within RG 128, the records produced by the House and Senate are maintained separately.

## G. Published Committee Records

### 1. Hearings

The committees of the Senate and House of Representatives generally hold three types of hearings: legislative, oversight, and investigative. Legislative hearings give members of Congress the opportunity to examine expert witnesses regarding policy issues that are before Congress. Congressional committees hold oversight hearings to assess whether federal legislation, mandated actions, or public policies are being implemented in accordance with congressional intent and the public interest. Investigative hearings allow Congress to inquire into the alleged wrongdoing of public officials or private individuals in situations that may require a "legislative remedy" or impeachment. The Senate also holds a fourth type of hearing, confirmation hearings, as part of its constitutional obligation to advise and consent to presidential nominees, including federal judges.

Until the latter half of the nineteenth century, Congress did not hold many hearings. In the late nineteenth and early twentieth centuries, Congress published verbatim transcripts of selected congressional hearings in the *Serial Set*. Since 1924, Congress has published selected transcripts of hearings and related documents through the Government Printing Office. Published hearings include witnesses' opening statements, transcriptions of testimony, exhibits, reports, correspondence, appendices, and other insertions made by witnesses and members of Congress. Each congressional committee decides which of its hearings it will publish. Unpublished hearings are available with the records of the legislative proceedings of the Senate and House of Representatives at the National Archives in Washington, D.C. The Congressional Information Service (CIS) and LexisNexis have also placed the records from most unpublished congressional hearings in a microfiche collection as well as a subscription-based "Congressional Hearings Digital Collection."

CIS and LexisNexis have published several indexes to the published and unpublished hearings of both houses of Congress: *CIS US Congressional Committee Hearings Index*, 41 vols. (Washington, D.C.: Congressional Information Service, Inc., 1981–1985), which covers 1833 to 1969; *CIS Index to Unpublished US Senate Committee Hearings*, 10 vols. (Washington, D.C., and Bethesda, Md.: Congressional Information Service, Inc. and LexisNexis, 1986–2005), which covers from 1823 to 1984; and *CIS Index to the Unpublished US House of Representatives Committee Hearings*, 14 vols. (Washington, D.C.: Congressional Information Service, Inc., 1988–2003), which covers from 1833 to 1936. LexisNexis continues to publish supplements to these series.

## 2. Published Committee Documents

Documents and hearings ordered to be printed by particular congressional committees are published by the Government Printing Office in a series titled *Committee Prints*. The content and arrangement of *Committee Prints* vary widely from committee to committee. Most of the documents included are working documents produced by each committee, such as drafts of reports, proposals for legislation, sets of statistics, legislative analyses, investigative materials, transcripts of hearings, and miscellaneous documents.

*Committee Prints* has not always had a uniform numbering system, and the documents and volumes may be arranged differently from library to library. The House of Representatives has not adopted a uniform numbering system for its volumes of *Committee Prints*; the Senate only adopted a central numbering system during the Ninety-Eighth Congress (1983–1984). *Committee Prints* are usually published in small quantities and may not be available at all federal depository libraries. Researchers interested in using early *Committee Prints* should consult the Congressional Information Service's *CIS US Congressional Committee Prints Index 1830–1969*, 5 vols. (Washington, D.C.: Congressional Information Service, Inc., 1980).

Since the late nineteenth century, most congressional committees have published a legislative calendar, which the Judiciary Committee publishes in conjunction with its executive calendar. Researchers can use these calendars to determine the final status of bills and nominations and to find lists of hearings (both published and unpublished).

## H. Records of Senate Executive Proceedings

The Senate's records of executive proceedings are composed of two series of papers: (1) presidential nomination letters and (2) nomination files. Until 1946, each of these series in Record Group 46 was arranged by Congress and thereunder alphabetically by surname of the nominee. Presidential nomination letters continue to be so filed. Since 1947, however, Senate nomination files have been arranged by Congress and thereunder by the committee to which the nomination was referred. Accordingly, researchers interested in judiciary-related nominations since 1947 should consult the executive records of the Committee on the Judiciary.

Nomination letters sent by the President to the Senate—including nomination letters for judgeships, court offices, and other federal posts—are arranged by Congress and thereunder alphabetically by the surname of the nominee.

Nomination files include letters and petitions from the public in support of or in opposition to the nominee. Most letters are addressed to individual senators or the chair of the Judiciary Committee. In some instances, letters sent to the President or other executive branch officials were forwarded to the Senate and are also included in these files. Some early nomination files are missing; noncontroversial nominees may not have a file. Beginning in the mid-twentieth century, nomination files also included transcripts of nomination hearings (both from the Judiciary Committee and its subcommittees), short biographies of the nominee, investigative reports, depositions, newspaper clippings, papers from earlier court decisions by the nominee, and letters and reports from bar associations. Researchers can consult George P. Perros, James C. Brown, and Jacqueline A. Wood, comps., *Papers of the United States Senate relating to Presidential Nominations, 1789–1901* (Washington, D.C.: National Archives and Records Service, 1964), for a list of judges and court officers for whom Record Group 46 has nomination papers. Nomination files are closed to public research for 50 years.

Since 1789, the Senate has maintained an *Executive Journal* that records the Senate's actions regarding the confirmation of presidential nominees and records the Senate's responsibilities related to treaties. The *Executive Journal* was first made public in 1828, when the Senate decided to publish its executive proceedings dating from 1789. Since 1828, the Senate has published its executive proceedings at the close of each session of Congress.

Many of the Senate's executive documents and reports are available in the *Serial Set* (see section L, below). Some of the early Senate executive documents and reports, however, were printed in small quantities and were not included in the *Serial Set*. The Congressional Information Service (CIS) has produced a 2-volume *CIS Index to US Senate Executive Documents and Reports Covering Documents and Reports not Covered in the US Serial Set, 1817–1969* (Washington, D.C.: Congressional Information Service, Inc., 1987), that allows researchers to search for printed Senate executive documents that were not included in the *Serial Set* but that may be available at the National Archives, the Library of Congress, or some other repository.

## I. *Records of Impeachment Proceedings*

Article I of the Constitution grants the House of Representatives "the sole power of impeachment," which is the first stage of the legislative process by which federal judges can be removed from office. When Congress receives a petition, memorial, member's motion, or other message requesting the impeachment of a judge, the complaint is referred to a committee to report on the case. Since 1813, most impeachment cases have been considered by the Committee on the Judiciary. The committee investigates the charges against the judge and may subpoena witnesses or hold hearings. After it has completed its investigation, the committee issues a report recommending whether the House should take actions against the judge. Sometimes the House "lays the report on the table," meaning it takes no further action. If the committee report recommends impeachment and the House adopts the report, the House draws up articles of impeachment, debates those articles, and then votes on them (sometimes the committee draws up the articles of impeachment and submits them to the House with the committee report). If a majority of the House votes in favor of the articles of impeachment, the judge is impeached and the case is sent to the Senate for trial.

Article I of the Constitution gives the Senate "the sole power to try all impeachments." The House presents the articles of impeachment to the Senate and selects "managers" to act as prosecutors during the impeachment trial. The senators, sitting as a court of impeachment, hear the proceedings and vote whether the judge should be convicted and removed from office. According to the Constitution, "no person shall be convicted without the concurrence of two thirds of the [Senators] present."

House impeachment records in RG 233 are filed as a distinct series within the records of each Congress. Impeachment records include a complaint against a judge (which usually takes the form of a petition, memorial, or congressional resolution), copies of court records from the case or cases out of which the complaint may have arose, correspondence from private individuals, a record of the investigation and proceedings of the congressional committee, and the committee's report on the case, which includes its recommendations. In some cases, judges under investigation also sent letters to the House committee explaining the circumstances surrounding the complaints.

The records of the Senate related to trials for impeachment are filed as a distinct series within Record Group 46 for each Congress. Senate impeachment records include orders, resolutions, proclamations for the opening of the court of impeachment, oaths, copies of the articles of impeachment, messages from the House of Representatives, motions, documentary evidence, subpoenas, lists of witnesses, exhibits supplied by the respondent and the House managers, the respondent's answers to the articles of impeachment, roll call votes on motions and on the articles of impeachment, and other printed materials. Impeachment files may include printed copies of the Senate's proceedings during the trial, as well as copies of the Senate rules for trying cases of impeachment.

Senate impeachment files usually include copies of the House's resolutions impeaching the judge and appointing managers to attend the trial in the Senate. Senate orders include orders calling the court into session and removing the judge from office. In some instances the Senate maintained a separate manuscript journal related to the impeachment trial, but impeachment journals are usually maintained with the Senate's legislative minutes for that Congress.

House and Senate impeachment records are closed to public research until fifty years after the close of the proceedings.

A listing of judicial impeachment investigations and unsuccessful proposals to initiate judicial impeachment investigations in the House of Representatives is included in Warren S. Grimes, "The Role of the U.S. House of Representatives in Proceedings to Impeach and Remove Federal Judges," in *Research Papers of the National Commission on Judicial Discipline & Removal*, vol. 1 (Washington, D.C.: Government Printing Office, 1993), pp. 117–38.

## J. Records of Congressional Debates

While the Constitution requires each house of Congress to keep a journal of its proceedings, the Constitution does not require Congress to keep a record of its debates. Nevertheless, in the early years of Congress, reporters took notes from speeches in Congress and published them in their newspapers. The House of Representatives allowed reporters to cover its proceedings from the very beginning, although the Senate did not allow the press or public into its chamber until 1794.

Between 1834 and 1856, veteran newspapermen Joseph Gales and William Seaton compiled and printed the debates of Congress from the First Congress until the 1st Session of the Eighteenth Congress (1789–1824) in *The Debates and Proceedings in the Congress of the United States*, 42 vols. (Washington, D.C.: Gales and Seaton, 1834–1856), which is more commonly known as the *Annals of Congress*. The compilers used paraphrased accounts of congressional debates that they gathered from newspapers that had covered the debates as they transpired, including their own newspaper, the *National Intelligencer* (Washington, D.C.). Beginning during the Second session of the Eighteenth Congress, and lasting until the First Session of the Twenty-Fifth Congress (1824–1837), Gales and Seaton published paraphrases of speeches and summaries of "the leading debates and incidents" in Congress in the *Register of Debates in Congress*, 14 vols. (Washington, D.C.: Gales and Seaton, 1825–1837).

In 1833, Francis P. Blair and John C. Rives founded the *Congressional Globe*, 46 vols. (the *Globe* and the *Register of Debates* overlapped in publication from 1833 to 1837), publishing "condensed report[s] of the proceedings in both Houses of Congress." Between 1846 and 1850 the *Globe* attained semi-official status in both houses of Congress, and beginning in 1851, the *Globe* used highly trained stenographic reporters to publish verbatim transcriptions of congressional speeches. Congress opted not to renew the *Globe*'s contract when it expired in 1873. Since that time, the proceedings and debates of Congress have been published in the *Congressional Record* (Washington, D.C.: G.P.O., 1873–).

Researchers can use the indexes and appendices to these congressional proceedings to locate debates related to the judiciary. Researchers can also use the House and Senate *Journals*, or the printed versions of bills and resolutions, to locate the dates of specific debates in the *Annals*, *Register*, *Globe*, and *Record*. These published proceedings also give researchers summaries and verbatim transcriptions of debates on articles of impeachment in the House of Representatives, and the proceedings of courts of impeachment in the Senate.

## K. Statutes

Once a bill becomes a law, it is published in the *United States Statutes at Large* (Boston, Little, Brown, and Co., 1845–1873; Washington, D.C.: G.P.O., 1875–). In 1874, Congress compiled the "general and permanent" laws of the United States into a single volume entitled *Revised Statutes of the United States* (Washington, D.C.: G.P.O., 1874). In 1878, Congress published a second edition that omitted obsolete laws and corrected errors from the first edition. Since 1925, Congress has regularly codified and updated the "general and permanent laws of the United States" in the *U.S. Code*.

## L. Congressional Serial Set and American State Papers

Congressional documents have been published in two sets of volumes, the *American State Papers* (1789–1838) and the *United States Congressional Serial Set* (1817 to the present). The 38 volumes of the *American State Papers* are arranged into ten topical "classes." Within each topic, the documents are arranged chronologically. The tenth class, "Miscellaneous," contains documents related to the federal courts, including communications and reports from the President, federal judges, the heads of the executive branch departments, congressional committees, and state governors and legislatures, as well as correspondence, memorials and petitions from individuals and groups. These documents cover many miscellaneous topics, including the organization, structure, proceedings, and jurisdiction of the federal courts. Researchers can also find materials related to appropriations for the judiciary in the third class, "Finances."

Since 1817, the House and Senate have published official documents and committee reports in the *Serial Set*. Committee reports often pertain to congressional investigations or proposed legislation. The *Serial Set* also contains other documents ordered by either house to be printed, including messages from the President, reports from the executive departments of the federal government (many of which touch on judiciary-related matters, as described in Part III), resolutions sent from state legislatures, petitions and memorials from private citizens, records and proceedings from impeachments, and papers related to the Court of Claims, including opinions, lists of judgments and dismissed claims, correspondence, findings of fact, and reports from the clerk of the court.

The *Serial Set* is organized by session of Congress, then by Senate and House, and then by type of document. The *Serial Set* contains various types of reports and documents, which are printed in separate volumes for each house and for each session of Congress. Each volume of the *Serial Set* is assigned a serial number that researchers can use to locate the reports or documents within that particular volume. Within each volume, the published documents are numbered consecutively (e.g., House Report 1 and House Report 2, or Senate Miscellaneous Document 1).

The Congressional Information Service (CIS) has compiled a 36-volume *CIS US Serial Set Index, 1789–1969* (Washington, D.C.: Congressional Information Service, Inc., 1975–1979), which allows researchers to search the *Serial Set* by subject or name or to browse the titles of congressional documents in the order in which they appear in the *Serial Set*. Since 1970, CIS has published a regularly updated *CIS Index* that catalogs House and Senate documents and reports, committee reports, and Senate executive reports, as well as committee hearings and *Committee Prints*, both of which are discussed below.

## M. Internet Resources

The Library of Congress has digitized most early congressional documents on its "American Memory" website (http://memory.loc.gov/) under the heading: "A Century of Lawmaking for a New Nation: U.S. Congressional Documents and Debates, 1774–1875." "A Century of Lawmaking" includes searchable versions of the debates and journals of the House and Senate, the *U.S. Statutes at Large*, selected bills and resolutions, the *American State Papers*, and selections from the *Serial Set*. Some of these are fully keyword searchable; others have only searchable indexes. The Library of Congress provides access to recent congressional materials at its "Thomas" website (http://thomas.loc.gov/).

Researchers can also access published congressional materials through subscription databases, including LexisNexis, Westlaw, and HeinOnline.

## N. Documentary Editions

Several published collections of primary sources document the interaction of the legislative and judicial branches of the federal government. Bernard D. Reams, Jr., and Charles R. Haworth compiled *Congress and* the Courts: A Legislative History, 1787–1977: Documents and Materials Regarding the Creation, Structure, and Organization of Federal Courts and the Federal Judiciary, 6 vols. (Buffalo, N.Y.: W.S. Hein, 1978), bringing together congressional hearings, reports, and other materials that reflect "congressional concern with the composition and structure of [the] Article III courts." These first six volumes relate to the establishment of the federal judiciary, the Supreme Court of the United States, the U.S. Courts of Appeals, the creation of additional judgeships, the federal courts of special jurisdiction, and proposed reforms to the United States judicial system. Since 1978, several supplements have been added to this collection, including volumes that pertain to the U.S. district courts.

The Documentary History of the Supreme Court of the United States, 1789–1800, 7 vols. (New York: Columbia University Press, 1985–2003) includes a wide array of primary source material from the first decade of the federal judiciary's history, including documents related to Congress. Volume One, Appointments and Proceedings, and Volume Four, Organizing the Federal Judiciary, include documents that discuss the Senate's obligation to give "advice and consent" regarding presidential nominations as well as Congress's role in determining the jurisdiction of the courts. See Chapter 3 for further discussion of the Documentary History of the Supreme Court.

The First Federal Congress Project, at George Washington University, in Washington, D.C., has published twenty of a projected twenty-three volumes of the Documentary History of the First Federal Congress (Baltimore, MD: Johns Hopkins University Press, 1972–). The volumes reproduce the House and Senate Journals, the Senate's Executive Journal, documents related to the histories of legislation and petitions, congressional debates, diaries and notes on debates, and correspondence. Researchers in federal judicial history can use these volumes to find information about the Judiciary Act of 1789, the location and jurisdiction of the courts, and judiciary expenses. The volumes also reproduce petitions, memorials, congressional committee reports, executive branch reports, bills, proposed constitutional amendments, original and amended versions of legislation, calendars of debate, and correspondence regarding a wide array of topics, including judicial appointments, judges' salaries, and legislation related to the courts and court procedures.

# Part III. Executive Branch Records Related to the Federal Judiciary

The Judiciary Act of 1789 established a system of federal courts that extended throughout the nation, but the statute created no central agency to provide for the judicial system's administrative and budgetary needs. For 150 years, the administrative responsibility for the courts shifted among executive branch departments. In the twentieth century, the Congress established independent administrative agencies for the third branch of government and instituted a more formal separation of powers. Each of the following executive branch departments and agencies has played a significant role in the administration of the federal judiciary, and their records reveal much about the operation of the federal courts.

# Chapter 9. Records of the Department of State

## A. Historical Note

As a kind of home office, as well as an office of foreign affairs, the Department of State was responsible for several aspects of judicial administration during the first century of the federal government. In an act of September 1789, Congress charged the Department of State with responsibility for the great seal of the United States, which was to be affixed to all civil commissions approved by the President. The Department issued the commissions, including those that authorized newly appointed judges to take the oath of office and hold court, and maintained records of judges' commissions until Congress transferred responsibility for judicial appointments to the Department of Justice in 1888. The early courts also relied on the Department of State to distribute printed compendiums of public statutes. In practice, the Secretary of State played the principal role in advising the President on judicial nominations in the early years of the government, and, although the Attorney General informally assumed this responsibility beginning in the 1850s, the Department of State maintained the records of judicial nominations throughout the nineteenth century.

## B. Archival Records

The records of the Department of State are in Record Group 59 at the National Archives at College Park, Maryland. The State Department's records related to the federal judiciary include general records, appointment records, and records related to presidential pardons.

## C. General Records

The general records of the State Department include correspondence, drafts of letters, ledgers, circulars for U.S. marshals and attorneys, and records related to the publication and distribution of laws.

From 1789 to 1950, the Department of State was responsible for the publication of U.S. laws. Initially the acts and resolutions of Congress were published in newspapers, but eventually they were collected into the *United States Statutes at Large*, which was published privately from

1845 until 1874, when Congress authorized the Government Printing Office to produce the volumes. Record Group 59 includes correspondence between the State Department and private publishers from 1789 to 1875, lists of newspapers in which U.S. laws were published, records related to the distribution to judges and clerks of court of the *Statutes at Large* and other books, contracts and receipts for printing, and transcriptions of the U.S. laws from the first twenty-four Congresses.

In the early nineteenth century, federal judges, court officers, and private citizens corresponded with the Secretary of State regarding matters that would today be handled by the Department of Justice. The State Department's collections of miscellaneous letters received (1789–1906) and domestic letters sent (1784–1906) include such correspondence— relating to judicial appointments, the misconduct of court officers, suits brought in the federal courts, piracy and prize cases, instructions to U.S. attorneys and marshals, claims, extraditions, pardons, and the violation of federal criminal laws. The correspondence in these collections related to appointments is not duplicated in the appointment files described below. In addition, the State Department records include bankruptcy returns from the district courts (1845–1846), returns from the district courts regarding federal criminal cases (1789–1827), correspondence regarding copyrights (1831–1834), and papers related to piracy and privateers (1813–1835).

The general records of the State Department contain several series related to judicial accounts, including letters to the President requesting the authorization of disbursements of appropriated funds under an act of 1823, and letters received from the Bureau of Accounts relating to the publication of laws and the accounts of U.S. marshals. The State Department also kept general and special ledgers (1820–1874) that detailed many Department accounts, including those relating to the extradition of criminals, the printing of U.S. laws, and the accounts of U.S. marshals.

Record Group 59 includes registers and indexes to the various collections of State Department correspondence. Researchers can also use published calendars to locate particular correspondents or letters from specific judicial districts. In the 1890s, the State Department published calendars of the papers sent and received during the secretaryships of Thomas Jefferson, James Madison, and James Monroe, as well as a *Calendar of the Miscellaneous Letters Received by the Department of State, from the Organization of the Government to 1820* (Washington, D.C.: G.P.O.,

1897). See Appendix B for further bibliographic information regarding these State Department calendars.

## D. Appointment Records

The State Department's appointment records include correspondence, registers of applications, Senate confirmations and rejections, acceptances and orders for commissions, lists, and miscellaneous records. Most of the appointment records related to the judiciary in RG 59 date from between 1797 and 1853, although some appointment-related correspondence and papers related to the issuance of commissions date until 1888.

Correspondence related to appointments include applications and recommendations for office, presidential nominations, letters of acceptance, resignations and declinations, and letters and orders suspending U.S. marshals and attorneys. The appointment papers in Record Group 59—which include correspondence related to all federal offices that could be filled by the President—are organized into groups that roughly correspond to the presidential administrations, with the earliest dating back to the administration of John Adams (1797–1801). Within each grouping, the correspondence is organized alphabetically by surname of the applicant or nominee.

The National Archives has prepared indexes to these collections of correspondence, listing the names of each applicant or nominee, the number of letters in their respective file, and other appointment files in which the nominee is mentioned. These indexes can be accessed at the various National Archives facilities or downloaded from NARA's online microfilm catalog at http://www.archives.gov/research/formats/microfilm.html.

The State Department transferred the appointment records from George Washington's administration to the Library of Congress, which incorporated the records within its collection of George Washington Papers. The Library's Manuscript Division has made these records available online at http://memory.loc.gov/ammem/gwhtml/gwhome.html (the appointment records are in Series 7 of the Washington Papers). Researchers interested in Washington's appointment papers may also wish to consult Gaillard Hunt, comp., *Calendar of Applications and Recommendations for Office during the Presidency of George Washington, Prepared from the Files of the Bureau of Appointments, Department of State* (Washington, D.C.: G.P.O., 1901).

Record Group 59 also includes indexes and registers of applications, copies of Senate resolutions confirming or rejecting nominees, copies of commissions for various offices (including separate files of temporary and permanent commissions), oaths of office, and lists of various federal appointees, including judges, marshals, U.S. attorneys, and justices of the peace in the District of Columbia. Other records related to judiciary appointments may be scattered in other series within RG 59.

## E. Pardon Records

From 1789 to 1853, the Secretary of State received petitions seeking pardon for criminals convicted in the federal courts. The Secretary of State and Attorney General jointly considered these petitions and made recommendations to the President regarding each case. In 1853, the task of reviewing petitions for pardon became the sole responsibility of the Attorney General, although the Secretary of State continued to issue pardon warrants until 1893.

The State Department's records related to pardons include petitions for pardon, correspondence, briefs, reports, pardons and remissions, requisitions, and drafts of pardons. Record Group 59 also includes catalogs, registers, and indexes that researchers can use to locate particular cases or types of crimes. Most of the pardon records in RG 59 date from 1789 to 1860, although the State Department kept copies of pardons and remissions until 1893.

Researchers interested in brief summaries of cases in which convicts petitioned the President for pardon between 1793 and 1853 should consult the Records of the Office of the Pardon Attorney in Record Group 204, which includes a set of abstracts of pardon cases that were handled by the Department of State.

# Chapter 10. Records of the Department of the Treasury and Related Agencies

## A. Historical Note

From the inauguration of the federal government in 1789 until 1849, the Department of the Treasury supervised the financial administration of the federal courts. The act establishing the Treasury Department in September 1789 gave the Department responsibility for disbursing all appropriated money from the federal Treasury and for receipt of all revenues of the United States, thus connecting it to the daily operation of the federal courts as well as to executive branch officials, such as customs officers throughout the nation. Further legislative mandates required all federal officials receiving public money to submit proper accounts. In 1820, Congress specifically instructed the clerks of the federal courts to submit to the Department of the Treasury, within 30 days of the adjournment of a court session, a list of all judgments and decrees to which the United States was a party, with the monetary amounts awarded for and against the federal government. Until 1849, when the Interior Department assumed responsibility for supervising judiciary accounts, the courts' accounts with the Department of the Treasury provided the only central record of the business before the lower courts of the federal judiciary.

After 1849, members of the judiciary continued to correspond with Treasury Department officials about salaries, additional funds for supplies, litigation involving the federal government, court fees, and other related matters. The Department of the Treasury also oversaw records related to the administration of judiciary accounts by the Department of the Interior, from 1849 to 1870, and the Justice Department, from 1870 to 1939.

## B. Archival Records

The historic records of the Department of the Treasury relating to the federal courts are maintained in several record groups, most of which are held at the National Archives facilities in Washington, D.C., and College Park, Maryland. The General Records of the Department of the

Treasury are in Record Group 56 at the National Archives at College Park, Maryland. Additional records can be found in RG 206, Records of the Solicitor of the Treasury; RG 217, Records of the Accounting Officers of the Department of the Treasury; and RG 87, Records of the U.S. Secret Service, as well as in a few other record groups that are briefly described at the end of this chapter. Many of the Treasury Department's early records were destroyed by a fire in the Treasury Department building in 1833, although some pre-1833 records have survived and are described in this chapter.

## C. Archival Records of the Department of the Treasury

This section describes the Treasury Department's general, administrative, fiscal, and claims records related to the federal judiciary. Subsequent headings describe the records of particular offices or agencies within the Treasury Department that worked with the federal courts.

### 1. General and Administrative Records

Record Group 56 includes several collections of correspondence between the Department of the Treasury and members of the judicial branch. The Department organized its correspondence into "series," which are arranged according to the office or department with which the Treasury Department was corresponding. Letters to and from members of the federal judiciary are kept in various collections within the "F" series.

The "F" series includes copies of letters sent by the Department to members of the judiciary (1833–1878) as well as letters received from the courts (1829–1899). Much of the incoming correspondence is from judges, marshals, and clerks and relates to salaries, court expenses, cases, the conduct of Treasury officials, counterfeiting of U.S. currency, the sale of seized property, bankruptcy, the arrest of criminals, court fees, the rental of court space, the construction of court houses, and requisitions for furniture and supplies. Some correspondents enclosed reports, asked questions about cases, sought information about the disposal of funds, transmitted information regarding bankruptcy proceedings, forwarded deposits, or explained the disbursement of public funds. A separate subseries of letters received from judges and court officers in the Southern District of New York, the Eastern District of Pennsylvania, and the District of Indiana between 1829 and 1833 includes correspondence related to the payment of government informers, judgments awarded by the courts, the rental of office space for court staff, and the proceedings in bankruptcy and customs cases.

Some correspondence files are arranged chronologically while others are organized by state and thereunder by judicial district. The Treasury Department created registers and indexes for most of its incoming and outgoing correspondence. Researchers can use these tools to locate letters from particular court officers or judicial districts.

Other sets of correspondence related to the judiciary within RG 56 include letters received from the Attorney General and other Department of Justice officials (1831–1910), letters sent to the Attorney General and the Department of Justice (1866–1878), correspondence and enclosures received from the Solicitor of the Treasury (1819–1905), and letters received from the Board of General Appraisers in New York City (1851–1910). Much of the Department of Justice correspondence in Record Group 56 dealt with federal court cases in which the Treasury Department had an interest, or regulations related to the payment of judiciary officers. Records and correspondence received from the Solicitor of the Treasury related to the many legal matters and federal court cases with which the Solicitor was involved, including cases between the United States and state banks, violations of customs and internal revenue laws, and other federal criminal cases.

## 2. Fiscal and Accounting Records

Most of the Treasury Department's records relating to judiciary accounts are held among the Records of the Accounting Officers of the Department of the Treasury in Record Group 217 at the National Archives in Washington, D.C. RG 217 includes ledgers, daybooks, journals, and correspondence from the mid-nineteenth to the early twentieth century that detail the accounts of court officers and the disbursing officers of the Department of Justice, as well as the payment of fees and expenses to court officials.

In 1789, Congress created the office of the Comptroller (later changed to the First Comptroller) to superintend, examine, and certify public accounts, to provide accountability in the spending of public funds, and to oversee prosecutions resulting from revenue officers' delinquencies or debts owed to the United States. The general records of the First Comptroller include letters received from the Secretary of the Treasury regarding accounts and claims (1801–1856), letters sent to court officers regarding the settlement of accounts (1839–1871), and abstracts of decisions relating to judicial accounts (1832–1850).

In 1876, the First Comptroller created the Division of Judiciary Accounts, making it responsible for the final approval of the accounts of judicial officers. The records of the Division include incoming and outgoing correspondence (1797–1917) with the Attorney General, the Solicitor of the Treasury, judges and other court officers, and members of Congress relating to judiciary accounts, cases before the Court of Claims, decrees in customs cases, and the salaries and fees of court officers. The Division also maintained abstracts of judgments in customs cases in New England (1830–1838) and abstracts of the fees of court officers (1842–1891).

In 1885, the First Comptroller created the Division of Territorial Accounts, which was responsible not only for supervising the accounts of territorial officials (including judges), but also the salary accounts of the Supreme Court of the United States, the U.S. courts of appeals, U.S. attorneys, and federal marshals. The Division's records, which date from 1835 to 1894, include registers of accounts as well as letters sent and received.

In the 1789 act establishing the Department of the Treasury, Congress created the office of Auditor to receive and settle all public accounts before transmitting them to the Comptroller. In 1817, Congress created the offices of four additional auditors and named the original auditor the First Auditor. The First Auditor maintained responsibility for settling judiciary accounts, and in 1868 established the Judiciary Division to audit judicial accounts. The records of the Judiciary Division include letters sent by the Division, emolument returns from court officials, and other miscellaneous papers related to judiciary accounts. The emolument returns, which span from 1842 to 1907, are organized by judicial office—U.S. attorney, marshal, clerk of court—and thereunder by state, judicial district, and then chronologically. Additional correspondence, registers, and audit reports related to judiciary accounts and salaries can be found in the records of the First Auditor's Miscellaneous Division, as well as in the general records of the First Auditor. The Judiciary Division was abolished in 1894, when Congress transferred the First Auditor's responsibilities relating to judicial accounts to the Fifth Auditor.

In July 1894, Congress made the Fifth Auditor responsible for settling the accounts of the Departments of State and Justice. In October 1894, the Fifth Auditor created the Division of Judicial Accounts to supervise the accounts of judicial officers and the Justice Department's disbursing clerks, as well as to ensure the payment of retired judges. The records of the Division include registers of letters received (the letters themselves are missing), letters sent, unprinted decisions of the Comptroller of the Treasury, and registers of the accounts of the disbursing clerks of the Department of Justice. The records of the Fifth Auditor end in 1921, when Congress abolished all of the auditors' offices and transferred their responsibilities to the newly established General Accounting Office.

The records of the Fourth Auditor (created in 1817) include records relating to prize cases, such as indexes to prize cases (1862–1873), abstracts of prize accounts (1815–1898), and other records relating to prize claims (1862–1903).

The Records of the Account Officers of the Treasury include a large number of "undescribed" items, meaning that they have not yet been incorporated into the appropriate sections of RG 217 and are not described in the preliminary inventory for the record group. Some records related to the judiciary can be found among these undescribed records, such as a judiciary ledger from the First Comptroller's Office that details expenses related to the work of the U.S. courts and the Department of Justice in the 1880s and 1890s. Researchers can find relevant materials among the undescribed records by using the National Archives' master location register at the National Archives in Washington, D.C.

### 3. Claims Records

In 1863, Congress authorized the Secretary of the Treasury to appoint "special agents" "to receive and collect" the property of Confederate citizens, property that was either captured by Union troops or abandoned by its rebel owners. In 1869, these agents were formally organized as the Division of Captured and Abandoned Property, with responsibility for furnishing information related to Southern claims to the Attorney General, Congress, the Court of Claims, and other interested parties. In 1881, the name of the division was changed to the Division of Captured and Abandoned Property and Lands, and in 1885 to the Division of Captured Property, Claims, and Lands. In 1887, the Division's responsibilities were turned over to the newly created Miscellaneous Division, and in 1906 to the Division of Bookkeeping and Warrants.

The records of each of these divisions, contained in Record Group 56, include incoming and outgoing correspondence as well as other materials related to cases before the Court of Claims. Correspondents include the judges and clerk of the Court of Claims, the Attorney General and other Department of Justice officials, claimants and their attorneys, agents of the Treasury Department, and other interested parties. Much of the incoming correspondence relates to cases before the court, investigations of evidence related to certain claims, appeals from the court's judgments, the loyalty of Southerners making claims, and the methods of taking testimony in claims cases.

The records of the Treasury Secretary in RG 56 include several series related to the Court of Claims. The "BE" series of the Secretary's correspondence includes 23 volumes of letters sent by the Secretary related to captured property and cases before the Court of Claims. The Secretary also kept a separate collection of letters and case papers received from the judges and clerks of the Court of Claims relating to the proceedings of the court, papers needed by the judges, the payment of Civil War soldiers' bounties, and the salaries of the judges and other court employees.

The correspondence files of these various offices and divisions within the Department of the Treasury are indexed and recorded in registers so that researchers can locate records related to particular litigants and cases. The records of the Division of Bookkeeping and Warrants and the Division of Captured Property, Claims, and Lands also contain dockets and case records, lists of claimants, case indexes, and statements of awards given by the Court of Claims.

## D. Records of the Solicitor of the Treasury

### 1. Historical Note

The act of 1789 that created the Treasury Department required the Comptroller of the Treasury to "direct prosecutions for all delinquencies of officers of the revenue, and for debts that are, or shall be due to the United States." In 1817, Congress transferred these duties to the First Comptroller of the Treasury, and in 1820 to the Agent of the Treasury. In 1830, Congress authorized the President to appoint "some suitable person, learned in the law," to be the Solicitor of the Treasury. The Solicitor assumed the responsibilities of the Agent as well as other duties related to the collection of debts that were owed to the United States.

The act of 1830 authorized the Solicitor "to instruct the district attorneys, marshals, and clerks of the circuit and district courts of the United States, in all manners and proceedings, appertaining to suits in which the United States is a party, or interested." The Solicitor could also require individuals to submit reports related to such cases in their respective judicial districts. In addition, the Solicitor possessed authority to issue instructions related to the collection of customs duties to court and customs officials, and to direct the U.S. marshal to institute proceedings against customs officials who were delinquent in their duties.

In 1870, Congress transferred the Office of the Solicitor of the Treasury to the newly formed Department of Justice. Over time, other Justice Department officials assumed most of the Solicitor's responsibilities. In 1933, President Franklin D. Roosevelt transferred the Office of the Solicitor of the Treasury back to the Treasury Department, stripping it of its functions related to litigation as well as its supervision of U.S. attorneys, marshals, and clerks of court. A year later, Congress abolished the position.

## 2. Archival Records

The records of the Office of the Solicitor of the Treasury are held in Record Group 206 at the National Archives at College Park, Maryland. RG 206 includes correspondence, legal opinions and briefs, case files, reports, and miscellaneous records. Additional records related to the Solicitor's acquisition and disposal of seized and surplus lands, dating from 1801 to 1943, are located in Record Group 121, Records of the Public Buildings Service, at the National Archives at College Park, Maryland. This section only describes the records found in RG 206.

### a. Correspondence

The correspondence of the Office of the Solicitor of the Treasury is divided into separate collections of incoming (1801–1934) and outgoing (1820–1934) letters. The correspondence received by the Solicitor is further organized by sender, with separate groups for letters received from the President, the various executive branch departments, and from "other sources." Each of the executive branch collections is then subdivided into series by sender within the department.

Much of the Solicitor's incoming correspondence relates to cases in which the United States was a party. Other letters report violations of various U.S. laws, including customs and revenue laws, crimes committed on the high seas, and the detection of counterfeit money. The Solicitor also received requests for information, instructions, and opinions on legal matters.

Letters received from the Attorney General, U.S. marshals, U.S. attorneys, and clerks of court are all filed with the letters received from the Department of Justice. These letters relate to any number of legal and administrative matters with which the Solicitor was concerned, including court finances and the payment of court officers, cases in the federal courts, the collection of debt owed to the government, claims against private individuals, counterfeit currency, and property confiscated during the Civil War. Some letters enclosed court records, such as indictments, transcripts of proceedings in cases, copies of docket entries, statements of the sale of property by U.S. marshals, and lists of cases before various courts. Letters received from U.S. attorneys, marshals, and clerks are organized by state, and thereunder by judicial district.

Many of the letters from the Departments of State and the Interior pertain to the appointment of court officers, to violations of federal law, and to cases before the courts. Letters received from the Departments of the Interior and the Navy include correspondence related to prize cases and confiscated property.

Under the heading of letters received from "Other Sources" are letters from Supreme Court justices, members of Congress, federal officials, and private individuals relating to litigation in the federal courts as well as to property being sold by the Office of the Solicitor. These letters are organized alphabetically by the sender's surname, and thereunder chronologically. Multiple letters relating to an individual person or case are often grouped together and filed under the last name of the individual or litigant.

Beginning in 1896, the Solicitor's Office organized most of its incoming correspondence into "case files" that include correspondence received from various government officials and agencies, as well as from private individuals, relating to a particular case or transaction. Beginning in 1910, outgoing letters were incorporated into the case files. The Solicitor's Office also kept a separate set of case files that arose from decisions of the Board of General Appraisers in New York City and the U.S. Circuit Court for the Southern District of New York.

Most of the Solicitor's outgoing letters are kept in a set of chronologically arranged letter books, dating from 1821 to 1934. Several other collections of the Solicitor's outgoing correspondence include draft copies of letters sent (1820–1911), copies of printed regulations and instructions for court and customs officials (1830, 1848, and 1870), and copies of form letters that were sent to newly appointed marshals (1849–1857) and attorneys (1849–1854). The Solicitor also kept copies of letters sent to U.S. attorneys, marshals and clerks of court relating to suits on duty bonds (1830–1843) and the sale of public lands (1830–1842).

The Solicitor maintained registers, indexes, and lists that researchers can use to locate particular correspondents within both the incoming and outgoing correspondence files. Most of the bound volumes of outgoing correspondence also include alphabetical indexes at the beginning of each volume listing to whom the letters within the volume were sent.

### b. Legal Opinions and Briefs

The Solicitor of the Treasury frequently gave legal opinions to Cabinet officers and executive department heads. The Solicitor's Office kept copies of these opinions, as well as some legal opinions issued by the Attorney General, the Chief Justice of the United States, Department of Justice officials, and court officers. The Solicitor also kept registers, indexes, and digests of these opinions, which researchers can use to locate opinions on particular subjects.

The records of the Solicitor's Office include a small set of briefs and memorandums (1903–1932); this set of records includes an index.

### c. Case Files and Suit Papers

The Solicitor of the Treasury kept "case files" related to the litigation with which the office was involved (1791–1929). These case files include copies of incoming and outgoing correspondence, reports, briefs, abstracts, affidavits, depositions, accounts, and enclosures related to cases before the federal courts. (The Solicitor's case files do not contain the official record of the courts' proceedings; those are maintained by the federal courts in Record Group 21.) The case files are organized by type of proceeding—bank cases, customs suits, land suits, Treasury suits, internal revenue cases, personal suits and judgments, *in rem* proceedings, and miscellaneous cases. In addition, the Solicitor's Office kept a record of proceedings related to the accounts of postal workers, suits in the charge of U.S. attorneys, records of insolvent debtors, and records of cases that were compromised (meaning settled out of court).

The Solicitor tracked the progress of court proceedings in various indexes and registers. These registers generally provide the name of the debtor or defendant, the court in which the proceedings were initiated, the final judgment or decree, miscellaneous remarks on the case, and on occasion the location of the case in the original court docket. Some registers and indexes are organized by state or judicial district, while others are ordered alphabetically or chronologically. Most of the registers cover a specific type of proceeding, such as Civil War confiscation cases, suits involving customhouses, appeals from the decisions of the Board of General Appraisers, and suits against banks.

### d. Reports and Miscellaneous Records

The Solicitor of the Treasury had the authority to require, from U.S. attorneys, marshals, and clerks of court, reports related to the commencement or status of suits in the federal courts. Included among the Solicitor's records are sets of annual, quarterly, and specially requested reports from these court officers, as well as reports from other officers (such as collectors of customs) and copies of reports that were sent to Congress.

The Office of the Solicitor kept many other miscellaneous records related to the administrative functions of the Office, including circulars, warrants, requisitions from clerks of court for supplies, oaths of office, and law books. The Office also kept many fiscal records, including records of deposits, debts owed to the United States, lists of bonds received from U.S. attorneys, registers of payments made to courts and court officials, papers related to the accounts of U.S. marshals and attorneys, ledgers and daybooks, and records related to salaries.

## E. Records of the Secret Service

### 1. Historical Note

In 1863, the Secretary of the Treasury placed the Solicitor of the Treasury in charge of the Department's efforts to suppress the counterfeiting of U.S. currency. Two years later, the Solicitor organized the Secret Service Division. Prior to 1863, U.S. attorneys and marshals had been the only federal officers responsible for the arrest and trial of counterfeiters. At various times the Secret Service participated in investigations for other executive branch departments; beginning in 1906, the Secret Service was formally authorized to protect the President.

### 2. Archival Records

The records of the U.S. Secret Service are in Record Group 87; most of these records are stored at the National Archives at College Park, Maryland. RG 87 includes agents' reports, correspondence, records related to the apprehension of criminals, materials related to confiscated property, fiscal and administrative records, judicial records, and miscellaneous papers.

The daily and investigative reports of Secret Service agents summarize the activities of the agents and their subordinates, often listing suspects and arrests, convictions and sentences, expenses incurred in the performance of the agents' duties, property that they seized, and correspondence that they received. The Secret Service also maintained a set of registers and monthly abstracts that summarize much of the information found in the daily reports.

The correspondence of the Secret Service includes several collections of incoming and outgoing letters, as well as registers and indexes of incoming and outgoing correspondence. Very little correspondence sent or received before 1905 has survived, although the registers contain abstracts of letters sent and received since 1863. Much of the correspondence deals with the detection of counterfeiters, the protection of the President, spies during the Spanish–American War, and special investigations. Most of the Secret Service's letters are kept in general correspondence files; however, a few specific sets of correspondence may be of interest to researchers in judicial history, such as the collection of letters received from U.S. attorneys (1879–1887) on the "usefulness and effectiveness" of the Secret Service's activities.

The Division's records relating to the apprehension of criminals include physical descriptions of suspects, photographs of criminals and suspects, "Wanted" posters, short histories of cases, record books of persons arrested and convicted, registers of counterfeiters and persons suspected of committing other crimes, and lists of suspected anarchists. The Division also kept "pardon and parole" case files (1926–1937) and investigation files (1920–1938) that include brief case histories and correspondence with the Attorney General, the Solicitor of the United States, U.S. attorneys, and other federal officials regarding the pardon of persons who had been arrested by the Secret Service. The Division's records relating to contraband and confiscated property include registers and indexes of counterfeit money and contraband property seized by the Secret Service, and inventories of property that had been used as evidence in federal court cases.

The Division's fiscal and administrative records include reports submitted to the Solicitor of the Treasury, employment and dismissal records, cash books, ledgers, payrolls, orders, circulars, and miscellaneous papers. The Division's judicial records include a record of actions taken in cases involving suspects arrested by the Secret Service (1931–1932), and a set of correspondence and opinions on legal matters received from the Solicitor of the Treasury and the Attorney General (1883–1915).

## F. Other Treasury Records of Related Interest

The National Archives maintains several other record groups that contain Treasury Department records that may be of interest to researchers in federal judicial history. Further records related to federal accounts can be found in RG 39, Records of the Bureau of Accounts (Treasury); RG 50, Records of the Treasurer of the United States; and RG 411, Records of the Government Accountability Office (known as the General Accounting Office from 1921 to 2004). The records of the Supervising Architect of the Treasury Department, which are held with the records of the Public Building Service in RG 121, are discussed in Part IV of this guide.

Congress created the Office of the Treasurer in 1789 to receive, keep, and disburse "the monies of the United States." The Treasurer's records in RG 50, which date as early as 1808, include incoming and outgoing correspondence, cash books, ledgers, journals, trial balances, and other fiscal documents; these documents are related to the work of the Treasurer, the detection of counterfeit currency, and captured and abandoned property. Record Group 50 is held at the National Archives at College Park, Maryland.

The records of the Bureau of Accounts, which date from 1775 to 1973 (bulk 1789–1948), document the disbursements of federal monies from prior to the Bureau's establishment in 1940 until its abolition in 1974. Record Group 39 is organized by executive branch department, with series of records related to disbursements for the Departments of State, Justice, the Treasury, and the Interior, all of which include information related to appropriations for the federal judiciary. These departmental series include correspondence, subject files, ledgers, warrants, appropriation journals, and other miscellaneous papers. In addition, RG 39 contains the records of the disbursing clerks of the Treasury, as well as papers related to captured and abandoned property. Record Group 39 is held at the National Archives at College Park, Maryland.

The General Accounting Office, and its successor, the Government Accountability Office, continued the work of the auditors of the Treasury Department when the auditors' offices were abolished in 1921. The records of the General Accounting Office, which commence in 1920, are held in Record Group 411 and document the federal government's efforts to maintain integrity in the fiscal workings of the government. To date, very few records of interest to judicial historians have been accessioned into RG 411, although researchers may find some materials related to the judiciary in the Accounting and Bookkeeping Division's series of letters documenting expenditures and account transfers for various federal departments and agencies. Record Group 411 is held at the National Archives facilities in Washington, D.C., College Park, Maryland, and San Bruno, California.

The records of the Internal Revenue Service contain records that may be of interest to historians of the federal courts. Record Group 58, which spans from 1791 until near the present, includes correspondence, tax records, assessment lists, ledgers, claims records, records related to seized property, reports of U.S. attorneys regarding actions in tax cases, records of tax suits, and other miscellaneous papers, many of which relate to the violation of federal revenue laws. RG 58 also includes opinions of the Attorney General, executive orders, transcripts of evidence in court cases, compromise dockets, briefs, and judicial opinions concerning the 1894 income tax. Most of the records in RG 58 are at the National Archives at College Park, Maryland; however, substantial IRS records are also held at the National Archives' various regional research facilities.

# Chapter 11. Records of the Department of the Interior

## A. Historical Note

In 1849, "An Act to establish the Home Department . . . to be called the Department of the Interior" created a new Cabinet department that assumed oversight of the financial administration of the federal courts. The act transferred from the Department of the Treasury to the Department of the Interior responsibility for the supervision of the accounts of all officers of the federal courts. Henceforth, clerks, marshals, and district attorneys submitted to the Department of the Interior all accounts of fees received by their respective courts and all requisitions for the advance or payment of federal money. Interior Department officials regularly corresponded with court officers about many aspects of the operation of the federal courts, including the rental and furnishing of court buildings, travel expenses of judges and court officers, and salary disbursal. The Department of the Interior closely supervised the financial management of each federal court and enforced spending regulations.

## B. Archival Records

The Records of the Department of the Interior, in Record Group 48 at the National Archives at College Park, Maryland, contain records related to the Department's work with the judiciary, including an 1849 register of applications for appointment as U.S. marshals and attorneys, letters received from the Court of Claims (1855–1880), records relating to prisons in the District of Columbia and the territories, and registers of letters received by the Department relating to the judiciary (1850–1855), although the letters themselves were transferred to the Department of Justice (see Chapter 12). The largest set of judiciary-related records in RG 48 comprises 42 volumes of letters sent (1854–1869); these letters are related to court expenses, the accounts of court officers, rental of court space, instructions for court officers, and the suppression of the slave trade. Many of these letters were sent by the Secretary of the Interior to judges, marshals, clerks of court, and U.S. attorneys.

Record Group 48 also includes correspondence and case files related to court cases in which the Secretary of the Interior was a party. Some of these records, which range from the mid-nineteenth to the mid-twentieth century, are organized by the court in which the proceedings were held, while others are organized chronologically or by type of case. Several of the largest collections involve correspondence related to the suppression of the slave trade and case papers involving American Indians. RG 48 also includes a collection of letters received from the Attorney General (1862–1880) relating to patent and pension cases.

The Department of the Interior established a Division of Finance in 1853 to oversee the payment of the "salaries of all the officers of the department and its bureaus, and all contingent and other bills . . . , and all requisitions drawn for the advance of payment of public money." The Division of Finance maintained ledgers that tracked congressional appropriations for the Interior Department, including appropriations for the courts and court officers. Judiciary-related subjects in the appropriation ledgers include the construction and repair of courthouses and prisons, the rental of court space, expenses related to juries, the settlement of the judgments of the Court of Claims, the printing and distribution of U.S. laws and Supreme Court reports, and the payment of the salaries of court officers.

Most of the Department of the Interior's records relating to its administrative responsibilities over the federal courts were transferred to the Department of Justice when the latter was created in 1870, and these records are now found in Record Group 60, the General Records of the Department of Justice, at the National Archives at College Park, Maryland. These records include letters related to judiciary accounts sent and received by the Department between 1849 and 1870.

The records of the Accounting Officers of the Department of the Treasury, in Record Group 217 at the National Archives in Washington, D.C., also contain Department of the Interior ledgers that detail the U.S. marshals' accounts (1855–1907), civil journals that give the dates and explanations of fiscal transactions (1849–1894), and letters received from the Secretary of the Interior (1849–1870) relating to judiciary accounts, the federal courts in the District of Columbia, expenses incurred by marshals during their work in prize cases, and the appeals of court officers from the decisions of the comptroller.

## C. Published Records

The annual reports of the Secretary of the Interior include information related to appropriations for the federal judiciary, judicial salaries, recommendations for the better organization and administration of the courts, and miscellaneous topics. The Secretary's annual reports are available in pamphlet and book form and also in the *Serial Set* as official congressional documents.

# Chapter 12. Records of the Attorney General and the Department of Justice

## A. *Historical Note*

In the Judiciary Act of 1789, Congress authorized the President to appoint "a meet person, learned in the law" to serve as Attorney General of the United States. The act directed the Attorney General to represent the United States in cases before the Supreme Court and to give legal opinions to the President and the heads of the executive branch departments upon request. The Attorney General joined the President's Cabinet as early as 1792, but the Attorney General's salary was only half that of the other Cabinet secretaries, and the Attorney General was not given an assistant or office space until 1818. Initially, Attorneys General were expected to supplement their income through private law practice, but in 1853 Congress made the salary of the office equal to that of the other Cabinet members. Beginning in the 1820s, several Presidents recommended the creation of a "law department" to be headed by the Attorney General, but this did not occur until the creation of the Department of Justice in 1870.

The Attorney General's responsibilities gradually increased between 1789 and 1870, sometimes by congressional mandate and sometimes by matter of custom. In the early years of the federal republic, the Attorney General offered legal advice to members of the executive branch and the Congress, but, because such opinions were not mandated by law, Attorney General William Wirt ceased giving opinions to Congress in 1818. In 1853, the Attorney General began overseeing the appointment process of federal judges and other officers in the judicial districts. In 1861, Congress gave the Attorney General "general superintendence and direction" over the U.S. attorneys and marshals. In 1868, Congress authorized the Attorney General to oversee all government litigation before the Court of Claims.

In 1870, the act establishing the Department of Justice continued and expanded the legal and administrative duties of the Attorney General, who was named head of the department. The act transferred from the Secretary of the Interior responsibility for supervising the accounts of the U.S. attorneys and marshals, clerks of court, and other court officers. The act also required the Attorney General to supervise the conduct and proceedings of attorneys representing the United States in the respective judicial districts, and to submit an annual report to Congress on the business of the department. In addition, the act authorized the Attorney General "to conduct and argue any case in which the government is interested in any court of the United States."

In the act of 1870, Congress created the position of Solicitor General "to assist the Attorney-General in the performance of his duties." Congress also brought the solicitors of the Treasury, internal revenue, and the Navy, as well as the law officer of the Department of State, into the Department of Justice. The Attorney General was still authorized to employ outside assistance for litigation, but over time the need diminished.

In 1888, Congress transferred from the Department of State to the Department of Justice responsibility for issuing commissions to federal judges and judicial officers, including U.S. attorneys and marshals. With the abolition of the fee system of compensation for marshals and U.S. attorneys in 1896, the Department of Justice's disbursing clerk began distributing appropriated funds for the salaries and expenses of federal judges and court officials. In 1914, the marshals of individual districts assumed the responsibility of paying the court salaries and expenses in their respective districts. This continued until 1934, when the Treasury Department became responsible for these disbursements. The Department of Justice also compiled statistics on the business of the federal courts for inclusion in the annual report of the Attorney General and prepared and submitted to Congress the judiciary's annual appropriation requests.

Congress established the Administrative Office of the United States Courts in 1939, drastically reducing the role of the Department of Justice in the administration of the federal judiciary. The Department of Justice continues to represent the government in civil and criminal litigation, and it retains its responsibilities for supervising U.S. marshals and attorneys, and for issuing judicial commissions.

## B. Archival Records

Most of the records of the Attorney General and the Department of Justice are included in Record Group 60 at the National Archives at College Park, Maryland. RG 60 is divided into two sections. The first section consists of the records of the Office of the Attorney General (1789–1870); the second contains the records of the Department of Justice (1870–). The records of the Department of Justice in RG 60 also include some materials that were transferred from the Departments of State and the Interior when the Justice Department assumed administrative responsibilities from those departments. RG 205, which is held at the National Archives in Washington, D.C., includes case materials and administrative records from the Court of Claims Section of the Department of Justice. The records of the Department of Justice related to presidential pardons are held in RG 204, Records of the Office of the Pardon Attorney, at the National Archives at College Park, Maryland. The records of the U.S. attorneys and marshals, in RG 118 and 527, respectively, are housed at the various regional branches of the National Archives.

## C. Records of the Office of the Attorney General, 1789–1870

The records of the Office of the Attorney General include legal opinions, correspondence, miscellaneous papers, records related to California land claims, the papers of the Solicitor of the Court of Claims, and some personal papers of the Attorneys General—all of these records are from the years prior to the creation of the Department of Justice.

The records of the Attorney General include papers related to the legal opinions that the Attorneys General furnished to the President and executive branch departments. These papers include original opinions, copies and drafts of opinions, bound volumes of opinions, and a record of the circumstances under which opinions had been requested. Most of these opinions were also published and are available in *Official Opinions of the Attorneys General of the United States* (Washington, D.C.: Robert Farnham, 1852–1858; W.H. and O.H. Morrison, 1866–1870; G.P.O., 1873–1996).

Correspondence files make up the largest portion of the Attorneys General's records. The correspondence received by the Attorney General gives a deep and unparalleled portrait of the life and business of the federal courts. Included are letters, reports, affidavits, and other types of documents received by the Attorney General, between 1809 and 1870, from the President, federal judges, U.S. marshals and attorneys, state or federal officials, and private citizens. Many of these letters deal with cases and lawsuits, the enforcement of federal laws, appointments and resignations, legal questions, the organization of judicial districts within the states, jurisdictional conflicts between the state and federal judiciaries, rules of civil and criminal procedure, and the caseloads and budgets of the federal courts. The incoming correspondence is arranged by state or judicial district and thereunder by type of sender (i.e., President, federal judges, U.S. marshals, U.S. attorneys, other federal officials, state officials, and private citizens). The Attorney General also kept a series of letters received from other federal departments and agencies (including the Supreme Court, the Court of Claims, the Solicitor of the Court of Claims, both houses of Congress, and the various departments of the executive branch). All of the correspondence received by the Attorney General from 1809 to 1870 in RG 60 has been microfilmed by Lexis-Nexis (see Appendix B for a list of relevant finding aids).

The outgoing correspondence includes letter book copies of responses to the incoming correspondence (1818–1870), letters sent to the Solicitor of the Treasury (1830–1842), copies of instructions to U.S. marshals and attorneys (1860–1870), reports to the President (1853–1858), and correspondence with the Secretary of the Treasury regarding internal revenue cases (1869–1870).

The miscellaneous records of the Office of the Attorney General include records related to the office's finances and employees, and papers related to cases before the Supreme Court in which the United States was a party or had an interest, including briefs, memoranda, and transcripts of records from lower courts.

The records of the Attorney General include a collection of papers related to California Land Claims. In 1851, Congress established a Board of Commissioners to settle private land claims based on previous titles from the Spanish or Mexican governments. The decisions of the Board could be appealed to a U.S. district court and ultimately to the Supreme Court, and in 1852 Congress made the Attorney General responsible for handling these appeals. The Attorney General's papers related to the land claims include dockets (1854–1858), transcripts of proceedings before the Board of Commissioners (1851–1856), case files (1853–1870), correspondence (1853–1870), U.S. district court opinions (1858), accounting records (1855–1870), and reference materials (such as newspaper clippings, memorandums, notes, and Spanish and Mexican laws, ca. 1813 to 1862).

In 1855, Congress established the office of Solicitor of the Court of Claims to represent the federal government in cases before that court. The Solicitor's records include letters received (1855–1869), drafts of letters sent (1857–1862), and case files (1855–1870), which include copies of the papers that were filed with the court. Congress abolished the office of the Solicitor in 1868, transferring the Solicitor's responsibilities to the Attorney General. Subsequent records related to the Justice Department's Court of Claims Section can be found in RG 205; these records are described below.

The records of the Attorney General's Office in RG 60 include a small collection of personal papers (1832–1868), most of which were letters received by Reverdy Johnson (Attorney General, 1849–1850) relating to Johnson's private law practice. Other letters in this series are requests for employment within the government, and case papers (1819–1860) from private cases in which someone from the Attorney General's office served as counsel.

The pre-1870 records in Record Group 60 represent only a limited amount of the Attorneys General's papers. Prior to the creation of the Department of Justice, many Attorneys General took their papers with them when they left office. Accordingly, researchers may wish to examine collections of Attorneys General's personal papers, which are held in libraries and archival repositories at various places throughout the United States (see Part V).

## D. Records of the Department of Justice, 1870–

The records of the Department of Justice in Record Group 60 are divided into two parts: (1) General Records and (2) Records of Officials and Organizational Units. Within this second part are the post-1870 papers of the Attorney General, the Deputy Attorney General, the Solicitor General, the Assistant Attorneys General, and the various divisions of the Department of Justice. The descriptions in this guide are limited to those records that relate to the organization of the judiciary or the Department of Justice's role in cases before the federal courts.

### 1. General Records

The Justice Department's general records include dockets and other case-related papers, legal opinions, correspondence, subject files, materials related to the administration of the federal judiciary, and other miscellaneous records.

The Department of Justice kept dockets (1885–1928) to track the various cases that it initiated in the federal courts. The dockets are grouped by type of case or by the courts in which the cases were tried. These include railroad land-grant cases, antitrust and interstate commerce cases, national bank cases, criminal cases, and cases before the district courts, the circuit courts of appeals, and the Supreme Court. The general records also include a docket related to other miscellaneous cases involving the United States; some of these cases were in the courts of foreign nations.

The general records of the Department of Justice include several sets of records related to the Attorney General's opinions, including letters requesting opinions, registers of requests, bound copies of opinions, and copies of the official volumes of published opinions. The Department also kept correspondence related to the publication of opinions.

The Justice Department's general records include several collections of correspondence covering judicial accounts, law enforcement, railroads and public lands, and other topics. Between 1870 and 1903, the Department maintained its incoming and outgoing correspondence in separate files. General letters received prior to 1884 are organized by sender (President, Congress, judicial district, private citizens, etc.) and thereunder chronologically. From 1884 to 1903, the Department organized its incoming correspondence into "Year Files" in which letters received each year were arranged by subject and thereunder in the order in which they were received. Copies of outgoing correspondence sent prior to 1904 are organized chronologically in several topical files. From 1904 to 1918, general incoming and outgoing correspondence was kept together and organized using a numerical filing system. Beginning about 1914, incoming and outgoing correspondence was combined and organized into subject files.

Researchers wishing to locate correspondence from a particular person or judicial district, or related to a specific subject, can use the various registers and indexes that the Department created to catalog its incoming and outgoing correspondence. These indexes and registers are part of Record Group 60 and can be requested at the National Archives at College Park, Maryland.

The general records of the Department of Justice include several separate categories of outgoing correspondence specifically related to the federal judiciary, including instructions sent to U.S. attorneys and marshals, letters sent regarding various types of court cases or legal matters (including bankruptcy proceedings and French Spoliation cases before the Court of Claims), and correspondence related to the administration of the courts in the various judicial districts. The letters in these series generally date between 1870 and 1905.

Prior to 1904, the Department kept recipient-specific letter books for correspondence sent to members of the executive, legislative, and judicial branches of the government, including specific books of letters sent to judges, clerks, and marshals. Most of the letters sent to judges and clerks pertain to lesser issues, such as leaves of absence or requests for documents, although some letters concern complaints of judicial misconduct, statutory interpretation, appointments and resignations, or the need for new legislation.

The Department of Justice inherited the Department of the Interior's correspondence related to judicial accounts and kept that correspondence, along with its own judiciary-related correspondence, in several distinct series within its general records. Incoming correspondence (1849–1889) is organized by state, then judicial district, and thereunder chronologically. Copies of outgoing letters (1849–1884), which are kept in letter books, are organized chronologically. These collections of correspondence document the executive branch's oversight of the judiciary's finances in the second half of the nineteenth century, dealing with such issues as the rental of courtrooms and office space, requests by judicial officers for extra funds, jury and witness expenses, the counterfeiting of U.S. currency, and requests for copies of laws or blank forms. Some letters also transmitted the bonds of court officers, the reports of prison inspectors, reports by special agents of the Interior Department on the condition of court meeting places, court records and opinions, instructions and circulars, and the accounts of jurors and legal assistants. Correspondents include judges, clerks of court, U.S. marshals and attorneys, members of Congress, various Cabinet members, jurors, and private citizens.

Judicial District Administration Files (1912–1938) contain correspondence between the Department of Justice and court officials relating to legal, political, and administrative matters in each judicial district. These files, which are organized by a subject–numeric system devised by the Department, include letters, memorandums, reports, transcriptions of conversations, and other documents related to numerous court-related topics, such as actions by the courts, caseload statistics, leaves of absence, fiscal requests, psychiatric services, and instructions to U.S. marshals and attorneys.

The Justice Department's subject files relate to investigations, litigation, and other activities in which the Department participated. Many of these files, which span the entire twentieth century, can only be accessed through a Freedom of Information Act (FOIA) request. These subject files cover a broad spectrum of the Department's work. Topics related to civil rights include voting rights, peonage, desegregation in public accommodations and schools, discrimination in employment and jury service, and the activities of the Ku Klux Klan. Many files relate to the violation of federal laws, including liquor violations, mail fraud, theft from interstate commerce, food and drug prosecutions, crime on the high seas, antitrust violations, customs violations, bribery, perjury, offences against public justice, and the killing or assaulting of federal officers. Other files have to do with war-related matters, patents and copyrights, elections and political activity, bankruptcy, public lands, immigration, and claims against the United States.

## 2. Records of Officials and Organizational Units

Record Group 60 includes subgroups of records created or collected by the various officers, offices, and divisions of the Department of Justice. These administrative records are organized by the collecting official or division and include correspondence, speeches, judicial records, appointment files, subject files, court decisions, records related to other federal agencies, and other miscellaneous papers. This section of the guide only describes the records of offices or divisions within the Department of Justice whose work related to the federal judiciary.

The post-1870 records of the Attorney General include correspondence, subject files, reports, personal papers, and miscellaneous records. The correspondence files include copies of the Attorney General's confidential letters to the President, Congress, federal judges, court officers, and departmental agents relating to litigation, appointments, proposed legislation, and the enforcement of federal laws. Separate correspondence files include copies of letters sent by the Attorney General's private secretary, records relating to requests from the public for information, and the personal papers of several Justice Department attorneys. Other records include a series of subject files, speeches, and miscellaneous records.

The records of the deputy attorney general (1930–1972) relate primarily to the appointment of federal judges. An appointment file for U.S. Supreme Court justices includes correspondence supporting or opposing nominees, copies of oaths of office and resignations, correspondence and memorandums relating to the justices, and newspaper clippings. The deputy's records include a separate file of endorsements for Supreme Court nominees who were not confirmed by the Senate. Federal Judgeship Candidate Files, which date back to 1960, include correspondence, FBI character reports, personal data questionnaires, bar association reports, newspaper clippings, and notes regarding persons who had been considered by the President for federal judicial positions but were either not nominated or not confirmed.

The records of the Solicitor General—to date these records are quite limited—include copies of outgoing correspondence (1909–1910) related to appointments, legislation, Supreme Court cases, and other matters. The records of the Solicitor General also contain an assistant attorney general's desk file (1918) that includes papers related to cases before the Supreme Court.

The records of the Administrative Division of the Department of Justice include the records of the chief and disbursing clerks, the general agent, the Division of Accounts, and the Statistical Section. The records of the chief clerk include correspondence (1882–1917) that reports on the work of the U.S. attorneys, marshals, and other court employees. The records of the disbursing clerk (1870–1924) include appropriation books, payrolls, records of vouchers and salary payments, and statements of accounts related to the finances of the judiciary. The records of the General Agent (1877–1923) include correspondence files, sets of instructions to examiners, reports, and other miscellaneous papers related to federal crimes, prisoners, and the Office of Indian Affairs.

The records of the Division of Accounts (1872–1939) include correspondence, examiners' reports, circulars, administrative files, and other papers related to leases for courtrooms, court fees and expenses, and the accounts of U.S. marshals, attorneys, and clerks of court. Examiners' reports may be of particular interest to historians of a particular judicial district as they provide detailed accounts—based on interviews and personal observations—of interactions between court officials, the use of courthouse space, record-keeping practices, litigation, possible fraud or misuse of funds, and other issues within the district.

The records of the Statistical Section (1931–1939) include correspondence and reports related to the amount and type of business coming before the various federal courts. Summaries of this statistical information can be found in the *Annual Report of the Attorney General of the United States*.

The records of the Department of Justice's jurisdictional divisions represent the various types of work conducted by the Department since the early twentieth century. These records include case files, correspondence, the personal papers of attorneys and employees, dockets, exhibits, and other miscellaneous files. The records of the Antitrust Division pertain to the enforcement of federal antitrust laws before the Commerce Court, the district courts, the Interstate Commerce Commission, and the Supreme Court. The records of the Civil Division relate to all of the civil proceedings in which the federal government was involved except for specialized fields that were assigned to other divisions. The records of the Criminal Division concern the enforcement of all federal criminal laws except for those specifically assigned to other divisions. The work of other divisions deals with civil rights, taxes, the use of public lands, claims for or against the United States, cost of living, insular and territorial possessions of the United States, Prohibition, the U.S. Board of Parole, and various war-related issues.

## E. Personnel Records

Record Group 60 includes records related to the appointment and service of federal judges, court officers, and U.S. attorneys and marshals. These records generally date back to 1853, when the Attorney General assumed oversight of the appointment of federal judges and U.S. attorneys and marshals. These records include correspondence, memorandums, orders, circulars, registers, lists, indexes, appointment files, and other miscellaneous documents. A few records, which date back to the 1840s, were transferred to the Department of Justice from the Departments of State and the Interior.

Most of the Department of Justice's personnel records relate to appointments within the judicial districts and the Department of Justice. The Department maintained appointment and application files for judges, U.S. marshals and attorneys, clerks of court, and other court employees. In most instances these records are organized by type of court, with separate files for the Supreme Court, district courts, circuit courts, courts of appeals, and courts of special jurisdiction. Appointment files for U.S. district and circuit courts are arranged by state and thereunder by judicial district. Appointment files include letters seeking appointment, endorsements, protests, letters of acceptance, oaths of office, resignations, and other related papers. The Department also maintained some separate files of correspondence, endorsements, and other papers related to appointments for various positions within the federal judiciary, including some collections related to nominees who were not confirmed by the Senate.

The Justice Department maintained many sets of lists, registers, and indexes that can be helpful for researchers who are seeking to know who served in various positions in specific judicial districts. These include lists of judges, marshals and deputy marshals, U.S. attorneys and assistant attorneys, clerks of court, and other judicial personnel. The registers also document applications, nominations, and endorsements for various positions in the Department and the federal judiciary.

## F. Court of Claims Section

The 1855 act establishing the Court of Claims also created the position of Solicitor to represent the U.S. government in cases before the court.

In 1868, Congress transferred the Solicitor's responsibilities to the Office of the Attorney General, and in 1870 to the Department of Justice. See Chapter 5 for discussion of the Court of Claims records.

## G. Office of the Pardon Attorney

From 1789 to 1853, the Secretary of State and Attorney General jointly considered petitions for presidential clemency, making recommendations to the President regarding each case. Beginning in 1853, only the Attorney General received and reviewed the petitions and made recommendations to the President. In 1865, Congress authorized the Attorney General to employ a "pardon clerk" to assist in the Attorney General's responsibilities relating to pardons. In 1891, Congress established the Office of the Pardon Attorney to assist the Attorney General in pardon-related matters.

The records of the Attorney General related to pardons have been transferred to RG 204, Records of the Office of the Pardon Attorney. The bulk of the Pardon Attorney's records are case files, which date back to 1853. Case files include applications for presidential clemency, letters of recommendation or protest, statements regarding the petitioner's character, correspondence from politicians or lawyers who had participated in the prisoner's trial, reports from judges and U.S. attorneys regarding the facts of the case (some reports include recommendations for or against pardon), statements from prison wardens and physicians regarding the applicant's behavior and health, copies of court records from the trial, briefs, transcripts of testimony, and the reports and recommendations of the Pardon Attorney and Attorney General.

Record Group 204 includes several series related to specific types of pardons, including pardons for political prisoners (1918–1933) and Utah polygamy cases (1882–1892). In addition, the Pardon Attorney kept copies of outgoing correspondence related to pardon cases, memorandums related to pardons, and miscellaneous papers. Researchers can locate particular cases, or cases from specific courts, using the dockets, record books, lists, and indexes included in RG 204.

Pardon records from 1789–1853 are located in RG 59, the General Records of the Department of State (see Chapter 9). On some occasions, pardon records remain with the records of the trial court in RG 21, and may even consist of a simple notation by the President on the original criminal case file. RG 130, Records of the White House Office, contains registers of presidential actions in pardon cases from 1869–1885 and

1907–1913. Pardon records are also kept with several types of military records, including RG 94, Records of the Adjutant General's Office, and RG 153, Records of the Office of the Judge Advocate General (Army). Most of these records concern civilians and military personnel who were tried before military courts during the Civil War and Reconstruction, although a few civilian court records are scattered in with them.

## H. Federal Bureau of Investigation

In his 1907 *Annual Report*, the Attorney General described the Department of Justice's need for a "permanent detective force." Within a year the Attorney General appointed nine special agents and a chief examiner to supervise all departmental investigations "except those to be made by bank examiners, and in connection with the naturalization service." In 1909, the chief examiner's division was designated the Bureau of Investigation "for the purpose of collecting evidence for the use of the Government in cases pending or about to be commenced in the Federal courts, and also for the purpose of making such other examinations and investigations as the business of the department might require."

In 1933, President Franklin Roosevelt's Executive Order 6166 established the Division of Investigation within the Department of Justice, combining the investigative responsibilities of the Bureau of Prohibition with those of the Bureau of Investigation. In 1935, Congress established the Federal Bureau of Investigation (FBI) within the Department of Justice "[f]or the detection and prosecution of crimes against the United States"; to protect the President; for "the acquisition, collection, classification, and preservation of identification and other records"; for the "investigation of the official acts, records, and accounts of marshals, attorneys, clerks of United States courts and Territorial courts, probation officers, and United States commissioners"; and for other investigative purposes.

The records of the Federal Bureau of Investigation are in Record Group 65 at the National Archives at College Park, Maryland. In addition to the records of the FBI, Record Group 65 includes correspondence, reports, and investigative materials from the Bureau's predecessor offices and agencies. Pre-1935 records include copies of letters sent by the chief examiner and the chief of the Bureau of Investigation (1907–1911), letters sent by the Attorney General regarding the Bureau of Investigation (1910–1912), the Bureau's correspondence with special agents (1908–1910), applications for appointment as a special agent (1917–1918), subject files, annual reports, the daily reports of special agents, memorandums, an index to federal court cases, and miscellaneous papers.

The investigative records in Record Group 65 are arranged by topic into classes. Many of the classes pertain to federal criminal investigations while others have to do with war-related matters, domestic security, or other issues. Researchers will need to consult with an archivist to determine whether the records they would like to use are open to public research. Some records in RG 65 have been classified by the executive branch of the federal government while others have been sealed by the federal courts.

Record Group 65 also includes the records of the Bureau of Criminal Identification (1896–1924) (most of those records have to do with fingerprinting); the records of the National Bureau of Criminal Identification of the International Association of Chiefs of Police (1897–1924); and the records of the American Protective League (1917–1919).

Researchers interested in federal investigative records may also wish to consult the records of the U.S. Secret Service in Record Group 87 (see Chapter 10), the records of the Bureau of Prisons in RG 129, the records of the Office of Alien Property in RG 131, the records of the Drug Enforcement Administration in RG 170, and the records of the Bureau of Alcohol, Tobacco, Firearms and Explosives in RG 436.

## I. Published Records of the Attorney General and the Department of Justice

Between 1870 and 1939, and in several nonconsecutive years thereafter, the Attorney General published statistical information regarding the volume and types of cases in each federal court, the expenses incurred by the courts, the amounts of judgments and fines awarded in cases in which the United States was a party, and other aspects of the federal judicial business in the *Annual Report of the Attorney General of the United States* (Washington, D.C.: G.P.O., 1870–1997). These volumes also contain summaries of reports by examiners and other Justice Department officials, as well as the Attorney General's recommendations for new laws and improvements in judicial administration. Annual reports since 1994 are available at the Department of Justice's website (http://www.usdoj.gov/ag/annualreports.html).

The Department of Justice publishes the names of federal judges, clerks of court, U.S. attorneys, marshals, probation officers, and other officials serving in the various federal courts in the *Register of the U.S.*

*Department of Justice and the Federal Courts* (Washington, D.C.: G.P.O., 1978–) (previously titled *Register of the Department of Justice and the Judicial Officers of the United States*, 1871–1900; *Register of the Department of Justice*, 1902–1912; and *Register of the Department of Justice and the Courts of the United States*, 1912–1976). The registers also indicate the times and places each court was held, the names of the counties composing specific judicial districts, and the allotment of Supreme Court justices to specific circuits.

Until recently, the legal opinions of the Attorneys General were published in *Official Opinions of the Attorneys General of the United States* (Washington, D.C.: Robert Farnham, 1852–1858; W.H. and O.H. Morrison, 1866–1870; G.P.O., 1873–1996). Recent opinions by the Attorneys General, and selected opinions of the Office of Legal Counsel, are available in *Opinions of the Office of Legal Counsel of the Department of Justice* (Washington, D.C.: G.P.O., 1977–), as well as at the Department of Justice's website (http://www.usdoj.gov/olc/opinions.htm).

## J. Records of United States Marshals

### 1. Historical Note

In addition to their duties as law enforcement officers, United States marshals have played an important role in the administration of the federal courts. The Judiciary Act of 1789 directed the President to appoint a marshal to serve in each judicial district for a renewable term of four years. The act required marshals to attend the sessions of the district and circuit courts within their respective districts and to carry out all lawful orders issued to them under the authority of the United States. Marshals carried out the courts' orders to make arrests, to provide for prisoners in federal custody, and to deliver summonses, subpoenas, and warrants. Under the provisions of the Judiciary Act of 1789, the marshal for the judicial district in which the Supreme Court of the United States sat was also responsible for serving the Court. A statute of 1867 authorized the Supreme Court to appoint its own marshal.

Congress authorized the marshals to adjourn sessions of the district and circuit courts when the judge or judges of those courts were absent. Marshals also provided protection for federal judges, jurors, and witnesses. In 1792, Congress granted marshals the same authority in executing federal laws as sheriffs exercised in carrying out state laws. At the same time that the marshals carried out their principal responsibilities in the federal courts, Congress and the executive branch assigned to them local administrative tasks, such as recording the census and receiving messages from foreign consuls resident in their district.

The marshals' administrative tasks within the courts arose out of their responsibility for the disbursal of all funds by the court, as provided by an act of 1791. They disbursed funds to pay the fees and traveling expenses of witnesses, jurors, U.S. attorneys, and clerks of court. Marshals also bought supplies for the judges and court officers, procured jail space for federal prisoners, hired bailiffs and court criers, and rented space for courtrooms.

The financial duties of the marshals required them to report to the Department of the Treasury all of the court's expenses and receipts of fees. In 1861, Congress placed the marshals under the supervision of the Attorney General. In 1956, the Department of Justice established the Executive Office for U.S. Marshals, and in 1969 the Department established the U.S. Marshals Service, with centralized authority over the marshals serving in the judicial districts.

During the twentieth century, and particularly after the 1939 creation of the Administrative Office of the United States Courts, the marshals' administrative responsibilities within the courts decreased while their role as law enforcement officers expanded. The marshals and their deputies continue to provide protection to judges, witnesses, and jurors, and they continue to execute the lawful orders of the federal government in the judicial districts.

## 2. Archival Records

The records of the U.S. marshals are held in several different record groups at the various regional branches of the National Archives. Initially, the U.S. marshals' records were grouped with the records of the U.S. attorneys in Record Group 118. Recently the National Archives created Record Group 527, Records of the United States Marshals Service, to hold the records of the U.S. Marshals Service as well as the pre-1969 records of the U.S. marshals. Many of the regional branches of the National Archives have transferred the marshals' records from RG 118 to RG 527, although a few branches still hold marshals' records in RG 118. Researchers will need to consult with an archivist to determine which record groups hold the marshals' records for particular judicial districts.

The marshals' records in Record Groups 118 and 527 are organized by judicial district. The earliest records date back to 1845, although most of the records date from between 1870 and 1920. Marshals' records include correspondence, docket books, records related to the marshals' fiscal responsibilities, appointment records, circulars, and subject files. Most of the outgoing letters in these records were written by U.S. marshals, although letters written by federal judges and U.S. attorneys are among these files. Some marshals also kept a separate collection of their correspondence with the Attorney General. Much of the correspondence in Record Groups 118 and 527 pertains to the capture of suspects, serving subpoenas, the progress of court cases, witnesses, federal prisons, and the marshals' accounts.

Many records related to the work of U.S. marshals are held with the records of the U.S. district and circuit courts in Record Group 21, although some of the regional facilities are moving these records from RG 21 to RG 527. Marshals' records in RG 21 most often deal with prize cases, seized property, bankruptcy proceedings, and the custody of prisoners. During the nineteenth century, U.S. marshals often shared office space with the clerk of court. For that reason, the official correspondence of the marshals will also occasionally be found among the records of a clerk of court in Record Group 21.

To date, very few marshals' records have been accessioned into Record Groups 118 and 527 (NARA only holds marshals' records from about a dozen of the ninety-four judicial districts in the United States). Many early records were lost or destroyed, and some official papers have remained in private hands (see Chapter 16). Researchers interested in locating the records of the marshals in a particular judicial district will need to consult the National Archives' online *Guide to Federal Records* (at http://www.archives.gov/research/guide-fed-records/) to see if such records are in the Archives' holdings. In addition to the materials in Record Groups 21, 118, and 527, researchers will find marshals' correspondence and reports in the records of the executive branch departments described elsewhere in Part III. The records of the marshal of the Supreme Court of the United States, in Record Group 267, are described in Chapter 3.

Researchers can consult the Historian of the U.S. Marshals Service at the Department of Justice regarding questions about particular judicial districts or individuals employed by the U.S. Marshals Service. The Historian maintains a file with information on more than 30,000 individuals who have served as marshals, deputy marshals, members of posses and guards, and other positions within the U.S. Marshals Service. The Historian can be reached by phone at 202-307-9114.

## K. Records of the United States Attorneys

### 1. Historical Note

The Judiciary Act of 1789 provided for the appointment in each judicial district of a person "learned in the law" to prosecute federal crimes and to represent the United States in all civil actions to which it was a party. Although the act did not specify who would appoint the attorneys, President Washington assumed the appointment power in September 1789. The statute did not confer a title upon these local agents of federal authority, but subsequent statutes and court decisions referred to them most frequently as "district attorneys." In 1948, the Judicial Code adopted the term "United States attorneys."

In 1820 Congress prescribed a term of four years for the attorneys, although it provided for their removal at the pleasure of the President. Until 1861, the U.S. attorneys received most of their direction from the Secretary of State, although the attorneys enjoyed a large degree of independence. An act of 1861 granted the Attorney General authority to supervise and direct the U.S. attorneys and required them to report their official proceedings to the Attorney General. Congress, when it established the Department of Justice in 1870, gave the Attorney General supervisory authority over the accounts of the U.S. attorneys.

The principal duty of the U.S. attorneys was to prosecute suits on behalf of the federal government. Like other officers of the federal courts, Congress occasionally gave the government's attorneys specific responsibilities related to the administration and operation of the courts.

No significant changes were made regarding the office of U.S. attorney in the twentieth century, but there was an increase in the degree of control exerted by the Attorney General and the Department of Justice over the conduct of U.S. attorneys in the field and over the appointment of assistant U.S. attorneys, who, unlike the U.S. attorneys themselves, have not been limited to four-year terms. In 1953, an order of the Attorney General established the Executive Office for United States Attorneys within the Department of Justice to serve as a liaison between the Department and the U.S. attorneys in the field.

### 2. Archival Records

The records of the U.S. attorneys, which are organized by judicial district and held in Record Group 118 at the regional branches of the National Archives, are more voluminous than the records of the U.S. marshals, but they are still far from complete. U.S. attorneys' papers have not survived from all states or judicial districts, and only a few districts have records from the nineteenth century. The records in RG 118 include incoming and outgoing correspondence, subject files, case files, criminal and civil dockets (with some pertaining to specific types of cases), grand jury records, and other miscellaneous records.

Case files, which make up the largest portion of records in RG 118, generally include correspondence with the Department of Justice and other federal agencies, memorandums, copies of court records, materials from FBI investigations, the U.S. attorneys' trial notes and working papers, newspaper clippings, exhibits, briefs, depositions, and miscellaneous materials. In some districts, U.S. attorneys maintained separate sets of "precedent" and "significant" case files, as well as case files related to particular types of cases, such as selective service cases, or proceedings against organized crime.

Grand jury records include transcripts of testimony, evidence obtained from wiretaps and other investigations, audio recordings, motion pictures, jury lists, witness lists, exhibits, and other types of material involved in grand jury proceedings. The grand jury records in RG 118 include materials from cases that went to court as well as from cases that never went to trial.

Records in RG 118 that are less than 75 years old must be screened by the National Archives before they can be made available to researchers. Recent U.S. attorneys' records are subject to a Freedom of Information Act (FOIA) request; however, grand jury materials are exempt from FOIA requests. Grand jury records that were not introduced into a case are perpetually closed until a judge orders them opened.

Researchers interested in finding papers related to the U.S. attorneys in a particular judicial district should examine the records of the lower federal courts in RG 21 as well as the correspondence files of the executive branch departments. During the nineteenth century U.S. attorneys often shared office space with clerks of court. As a result, the official records of U.S. attorneys will occasionally be found among the records of a clerk in Record Group 21. Some early U.S. attorneys retained their official papers at the end of their terms of service. Researchers can search for U.S. attorneys' manuscript collections in repositories outside of the National Archives system, many of which include both personal correspondence and official records (see Chapter 16).

# Part IV. Records Related to Federal Courthouses

## Introduction

From the inauguration of the federal government until the mid-nineteenth century, federal courts met in county courthouses, city halls, state capitols, and other public buildings, as well as in hotels, taverns, and attorneys' offices. Only in the second half of the nineteenth century did the federal government provide dedicated space for federal courts to meet. From 1852 until 1939, the construction of most nonmilitary federal buildings, including courthouses, was under the direction of the Office of the Supervising Architect in the Treasury Department. Before 1852, most government building projects were for customhouses, warehouses, and marine hospitals—all facilities under the jurisdiction of the Treasury Department. In an effort to coordinate the growing number of federal building projects, Secretary of the Treasury Thomas Corwin, in March 1852, selected architect Ammi B. Young to manage the Department's work in the construction and maintenance of public buildings. By the end of the year Young was known as the "Supervising Architect." By 1863, the Supervising Architect had taken control of building projects under the authority of the Treasury Department.

In June 1933, President Franklin D. Roosevelt issued Executive Order 6166, which changed the name of the Office of the Supervising Architect to the Public Works Branch and transferred it to the new Procurement Division of the Department of the Treasury. The order divided the administrative responsibilities for the maintenance of public buildings among the Treasury Department, the Postal Service, and the National Park Service, each of which had supervisory control over the maintenance of different buildings in which the federal courts met. In 1936, the Public Works Branch was renamed the Public Buildings Branch.

In 1939, Congress transferred the Public Buildings Branch from the Treasury Department to the Federal Works Agency, where it became part of the Public Buildings Administration. The former assistant director of the Procurement Division of the Treasury Department became the Commissioner of Public Buildings, and the Supervising Architect and Supervising Engineer served as his subordinates. Congress also transferred the

National Park Service's responsibilities for the administration of public buildings to the Public Works Administration.

Congress, in the Federal Property and Administrative Services Act of 1949, abolished the Federal Works Agency, the Public Buildings Administration, and the offices of the Commissioner of Public Buildings, the Federal Works Administrator, and the Assistant Federal Works Administrator, transferring their responsibilities to the newly established General Services Administration (GSA).

By 1950, the Public Buildings Service had been established within the GSA to select sites and acquire land for public buildings and to oversee the design, construction, extension, maintenance, and repair of public buildings. Since 1949, most public buildings have been designed by private architects, with the GSA providing administrative oversight of construction and maintenance of the buildings. In 1956, the title of Supervising Architect was changed to Assistant Commissioner for Design and Construction, a position that still exists.

Researchers interested in further discussion of the history of public buildings in the United States should consult Antoinette J. Lee, *Architects to the Nation: The Rise and Decline of the Supervising Architect's Office* (New York: Oxford University Press, 2000). Part IV of this guide directs researchers to archival records and photographic images of court meeting places that are held at the National Archives, the Library of Congress, and other libraries and archival repositories.

# Chapter 13. NARA Records Related to Federal Courthouses

Several record groups at the National Archives provide insight into the construction and maintenance of federal buildings and courthouses. The records of the executive branch departments that had administrative responsibilities over the judiciary include correspondence related to the design and construction of public buildings, the leasing of court space, funds for the improvement of federal buildings, and other related matters. Most of these records are Treasury-related, although the State, Interior, and Justice Departments also maintained such correspondence (see Part III). The largest quantity of records related to courthouses and court meeting places is available in the Records of the Public Buildings Service in Record Group 121.

## A. *Records of the Public Buildings Service*

The records of the Public Buildings Service in Record Group 121 at the National Archives at College Park, Maryland, include correspondence, fiscal and design records, maps, motion pictures, photographs, and miscellaneous letters related to the construction of public buildings by the Office of the Supervising Architect in the Department of the Treasury, as well as those constructed by the Public Buildings Service.

Record Group 121 includes several series of outgoing correspondence, including letters sent by the Secretary of the Treasury related to public buildings (1851–1863), letters sent by the Supervising Architect and his staff (1862–1930), and letters sent from the office of the architect of the federal building in Chicago (1896–1903). Much of this correspondence was sent to elected officials, the Attorney General, customs officials, architects, custodians, disbursing officers, contractors, and construction firms concerning the acquisition of sites, the construction or repair of public buildings, the sale of old buildings, maintenance issues, and other fiscal and contractual matters. Most of these correspondence files are organized chronologically; however, several duplicate sets of the outgoing correspondence are organized by place of construction. The Office of the Supervising Architect also created indexes and registers of its outgoing correspondence, and researchers can use these indexes and registers to search for correspondence related to a specific building, city, or person.

The incoming correspondence of the Office of the Supervising Architect includes two series of letters received. The first series covers the period from 1843 to 1910, the second from 1910 to 1939. The correspondence in the 1843 to 1910 series is arranged alphabetically by city, then by building name, and thereunder by date. The records in the 1910 to 1939 series are organized by state, then city, then building, and then chronologically. The records related to some cities or buildings comprise only a few folders, while those for some buildings fill more than twenty boxes. The correspondence for most buildings predates the construction of the building (except in cases where the building was completed prior to 1843) and extends through the use of the building by the federal government.

The Office of the Supervising Architect received much of its correspondence from members of Congress and other elected officials, local building commissions, construction companies, architects and architectural firms, custodians and other employees in federal buildings, and private individuals. Much of the correspondence relates to the acquisition of sites and the construction of new federal buildings, as well as to the alteration, maintenance, and repair of existing federal buildings. Letters from local officials often described their city's or state's need for a new public building. Clerks and other court officers often relayed their needs to the Supervising Architect as his office was preparing plans for a new courthouse or public building.

These incoming correspondence files include synopses of bids as well as the bids themselves, copies of congressional bills and laws related to the acquisition of sites and construction, reports on the condition of public buildings, correspondence related to construction or repairs, plats of sites offered and their prices, letters from winning bidders trying to renege on their contracts, letters from court officers enclosing receipts and bills, newspaper clippings, and other miscellaneous papers. Many letters also enclosed maps, blueprints, drawings, designs, and abstracts of titles to land.

On occasion, the Supervising Architect sent questionnaires to local postmasters and custodians of public buildings. The responses to these questionnaires, which are filed with the Supervising Architect's incoming correspondence, include descriptions of judges' chambers and court offices, as well as information about the number of people employed by each court officer. Some answers gave further demographic details about the employees in public buildings, such as how many women worked in particular facilities. The incoming correspondence files also include materials related to personnel disputes, such as complaints and explanations, sworn statements, and documentary evidence.

A third series of letters received from 1933 to 1945 documents the operation and maintenance of courthouses and other federal buildings by the National Park Service (1933 to 1939) and the Public Buildings Administration (1939 to 1945). These files include correspondence, telegrams, memorandums, newspaper clippings, blueprints, maps, invitations for bids on various projects, building inspection reports, and miscellaneous documents. Correspondents include the National Park Service, the Federal Works Agency, the Public Buildings Administration, the Treasury Department's Division of Disbursement, the Department of Justice, the Secretary of the Interior, and building managers and custodians. Subjects covered include building maintenance and repairs, personnel matters, operational expenses, fires, art and murals painted under the Federal Works of Art Project (often with enclosed photographs), and requisitions for furniture and office supplies.

The Office of the Supervising Architect annually compiled registers of the correspondence it received between 1857 and 1901. These registers include the dates that letters were sent and received, the name of the sender, and a brief description of the contents of the letter. Each volume is arranged alphabetically by city, then by correspondent or building, and thereunder chronologically. Researchers can use these registers to locate correspondence from particular persons or time periods, or to locate correspondence related to specific cities or buildings.

The Supervising Architect's Office kept several series of drawings, plans, and specifications related to historic federal buildings, many of which had been sold or demolished. A specifications file (1840–1943)—which is arranged alphabetically by state, then city, then building—details construction specifications for the plumbing, heating, painting, electrical wiring, and other repairs that had to be done to public buildings. The National Archives has consolidated the Office's drawings, tracings, blueprints, site plans, elevations, and plats into a "Consolidated File of Architectural Drawings of Public Buildings" (1833–1974), which is available in the Cartographic and Architectural Records Section of the National Archives at College Park, Maryland.

Record Group 121 includes several series of miscellaneous records relating to the overall operations of the Office of the Supervising Architect. These records, which date from 1854 to 1940, were retained as samples of the original records, most of which were destroyed at some point between the time that the government had finished using them and the time that they were organized by the National Archives. Included in these series are a register of proposals by contractors (1900–1902), a register of bonds of contractors performing work on public buildings (1889–1897), construction contracts (1854–1860), contract dockets (1882–1892), inspection files (1935–1940), miscellaneous ledgers (1816–1929), appointment books (1900–1902), and other assorted records.

The records in RG 121 of the Fine Arts Section of the Public Buildings Administration, which had been established in the Treasury Department in 1934 and existed until 1943, include correspondence, reports, memorandums, case files, proposals, and miscellaneous materials related to the installation of murals, sculptures, and other artwork in federal buildings. The correspondence files include letters received from and copies of letters sent to artists, architects, elected officials, federal agencies, the heads and employees of the Fine Arts Section, and other individuals. Several other topical correspondence files include series of correspondence with artists concerning competitions and projects (1939–1942), artists' answers to technical questionnaires (1936–1938), and letters received regarding completed works of art (1935–1942). The Fine Arts Section's case files (1934–1943) include letters, memorandums, and other papers relating to the design and installation of artwork in public buildings.

The photographic records of the Office of the Supervising Architect and the Public Buildings Service are described in Chapter 15.

## B. Records of the Department of the Treasury

Prior to the establishment of the Office of the Supervising Architect and the later Public Buildings Service, federal courts rented offices and court space in the cities and towns in which they were authorized to meet. The records of the Treasury Department include correspondence and fiscal papers related to the rental of court space during the first century of the federal judiciary's existence.

The General Records of the Department of the Treasury, in Record Group 56 at the National Archives at College Park, Maryland, include several series of correspondence related to courthouses, the construction of public buildings, employees in federal buildings, and the rental of courtrooms and office space for members of the judiciary. As described in Chapter 10, the Treasury Department organized its incoming and outgoing correspondence into lettered series according to the office or department with which the Treasury Department was corresponding. Most of the Department's correspondence files are arranged in chronological order, but the Department kept indexes and registers of its incoming and outgoing correspondence that researchers can use to locate correspondence with particular individuals.

The "F" series, which includes letters sent to members of the judiciary (1829–1878) and correspondence received from members of the judiciary (1829–1848), includes incoming letters from judges, clerks, and marshals, and the Treasury Department's responses, regarding the district and circuit courts' need for adequate court space, the rental of courtrooms and offices for court personnel, and the purchase of furniture, office supplies, and books. Much of the correspondence has to do with the purchase or repair of public buildings in the judicial districts, as well as requisitions for surplus money to cover unexpected expenses.

The "M" series (1878–1916) in Record Group 56 consists of letters sent by the Office of the Supervising Architect to members of the executive branch, Congress, construction companies, employees in federal buildings, and private individuals. Much of this correspondence pertains to the construction, maintenance, and repair of public buildings, including letters related to contracts and financing, appropriations, and the hiring of custodial staff. The "P" series (1878–1910) includes similar types of correspondence sent from the Office of the Chief Clerk and Superintendent of the Treasury Building.

Many other series in Record Group 56 include correspondence and papers related to the construction, maintenance, repair, furnishing, and sale of public buildings. These include the "E" series (1806–1874), which consists of outgoing correspondence and reports sent to members of Congress; the "GB" series (1877–1878), which includes copies of outgoing letters sent to the disbursing agents and custodial staff of federal buildings throughout the United States; and the "K" series (1789–1878), which includes miscellaneous letters sent and received, some of which related to the construction and maintenance of public buildings. The "K" series also includes a subset of records related to the construction of customhouses and other federal structures (1833–1849), but only one building in this subseries (the customhouse in Wilmington, N.C.) served as a meeting place for the federal courts. The "QN" series, which consists of outgoing correspondence related to employees in public buildings (1871–1878), includes copies of letters sent to construction and custodial staff at federal buildings relating to personnel actions, repairs, maintenance, salaries, and other expenses. The "OR" series (1861–1878) includes correspondence that was sent to other Treasury Department officials regarding the repair of public buildings. Some letters sent by the Division of Appointments, in the "A" series (1878–1902), also dealt with the appointment of custodial personnel.

The Secretary of the Treasury maintained several series of records, dating from 1853 to 1911, related to employment and personnel matters within the Office of the Supervising Architect and at various construction sites. The Secretary's correspondents included the Supervising Architect, applicants for positions, local politicians, members of Congress, construction firms, and other employees at construction sites. The Secretary also maintained lists, registers, and monthly reports related to employees in the Office of the Supervising Architect and in various public buildings, as well as records of payments to custodians and janitors, and oaths of office for persons employed in public buildings.

The Treasury Department's records include several other sets of correspondence that are not included in the lettered series, and some of these sets of correspondence relate to construction and maintenance expenses. These include several sets of letters received from other departments of the executive branch, letters received from members of Congress (1836–1910), and letters received from the Supervising Architect (1858–1910). Another series consists of letters received by the Superintendent of Construction (1903–1904). The Secretary also maintained a descriptive volume (1901–1918) relating to courthouses and other public buildings.

The Records of the Accounting Officers of the Department of the Treasury, in Record Group 217 at the National Archives in Washington, D.C., include correspondence, contracts, reports, and other accounting records related to federal buildings and courthouses. The records of the Register of the Treasury include various ledgers (1840–1909) that show the expenses of disbursing officers at various public buildings, as well as of court officers in the various judicial districts. The records of the First Comptroller include proposals and contracts for the construction of public buildings (1852–1901). The Office of the First Auditor kept a register of accounts for the rental of courtrooms (1892–1894), registers of accounts for public buildings (1870–1911), and a register of payments made on contracts for public buildings (1890–1894), as well as the settled accounts themselves and correspondence related to judiciary accounts and the use of public buildings.

Several other collections of Treasury records contain materials related to court meeting places. The records of the Bureau of Accounts (Treasury) in Record Group 39 at the National Archives at College Park,

Maryland, include appropriation ledgers for public buildings (1911–1939), registers of expenditures for the construction and maintenance of public buildings (ca. 1800–1870), and lists of maintenance employees in federal buildings (ca. 1877–1881). The records of the Solicitor of the Treasury, in Record Group 206 at the National Archives at College Park, Maryland, include correspondence and other materials related to cases in which the federal government was defrauded during the construction of public buildings.

The records of the Treasury Department are more fully described in Chapter 10 of this guide.

## C. Records of the General Services Administration

To date, few records related to federal courthouses have been accessioned from the General Services Administration into Record Group 269. Many of the records in RG 269 are "undescribed," meaning that they are available to researchers at the National Archives at College Park, Maryland, but they have not yet been described in a preliminary inventory or in the National Archives' Archival Research Catalog (ARC). In order to locate relevant records, researchers must read through NARA's master location register for the record group, which is available in the research room at the National Archives at College Park, Maryland.

Record Group 269 includes files related to federal buildings and properties, the general subject files of the GSA administrators, the central files of the Office of the Administrator, issuance case files, liquidation records that were transferred from the Reconstruction Finance Corporation, records related to the financial and administrative management of federal buildings, congressional correspondence, inventory listings of property owned by the United States, and the records of the Federal Building Fund of the Public Buildings Service.

The Office of the Administrator's subject files and central files include memorandums, as well as copies of incoming and outgoing correspondence between the GSA and the executive branch departments, the courts, Congress, architects, and other parties; this correspondence is related to the construction, maintenance, repair, and disposal of federal buildings and property, personnel and employment matters, supplies and equipment, budgets and appropriations, security matters, and other relevant issues.

The GSA's records relating to financial and administrative management include the files of the Administrator and other GSA employees, as well as a Public Buildings Service file that includes correspondence, training materials for new employees, copies of reports, and published guidelines for the design and construction of public buildings. Letters in the congressional correspondence file (1970–1973) pertain to, among other things, the construction and repair of federal buildings and courthouses within the congress member's state or district. The records of the Federal Building Fund of the Operations Division of the Public Buildings Service include legal files, correspondence, and memorandums related to the purchase, contracting, and construction of public buildings and lands between 1972 and 1979.

## D. Other Records at the National Archives

The records of the Department of the Interior in Record Group 48 include letters, drawings, plats, financial papers, and other documents related to the purchase of the Charleston Club House, in Charleston, South Carolina, for use as a courthouse. These papers date from 1867 to 1895. The forty-two volumes of letters that the Department of the Interior sent concerning the judiciary (1854–1869), which are more fully described in Chapter 11, also include information regarding the rental, purchase, repair, and fitting out of courtrooms and court office space.

The records of the Administrative Office of the United States Courts, in Record Group 116 at the National Archives in Washington, D.C., include a file of "Records Relating to Site and Facilities, 1940–1958." This file, which is arranged in reverse chronological order, includes incoming and outgoing correspondence, memorandums, reports, and other assorted papers related to the use of space in federal courthouses, needed repairs, and other related subjects. Much of the correspondence in this file pertains to maintenance work required for the Supreme Court building in Washington, D.C.

Researchers should be aware of several other record groups related to public building projects, although these record groups do not include many records related specifically to federal courthouses: RG 28, the Records of the Post Office Department; RG 79, the Records of the National Park Service; RG 135, the Records of the Public Works Administration; RG 162, the General Records of the Federal Works Agency; and RG 515, the Records of the American Engineering Record Division, which includes the records of the Historic American Buildings Survey (HABS, described in Chapters 14 and 15). Most of the materials in these record groups are available at the National Archives at College Park, Maryland.

# Chapter 14. Other Federal Resources for Research on Courthouses

This chapter directs researchers to resources outside of the National Archives system that may be useful for conducting research on the historic meeting places of the federal courts or on the history of a particular courthouse.

## A. *Historic American Buildings Survey*

The Library of Congress's Prints and Photographs Division houses the reports of the Historic American Buildings Survey (HABS). HABS is a project of the National Park Service and the Library of Congress that documents American architectural achievements. Begun in 1933, the program has made reports on more than 38,000 structures in the United States, including many federal buildings and courthouses.

HABS reports vary greatly in the information they include. Generally, HABS reports include data pages with construction dates (and date razed, when applicable), architects' names, dates of alterations and extensions, lists of owners, names of contracting firms, the building's location, and a brief survey of its historical and architectural significance. Many HABS reports include interior and exterior photographs of each building, captions to accompany the photographs, and sketches of the floor plans and exterior of the building. HABS reports also include bibliographies of primary and secondary resources that researchers can use to locate other materials related to the site.

The Prints and Photographs Division of the Library of Congress has digitized most of its collection of HABS reports and placed it online through both the Prints and Photographs Division catalog (http://www.loc.gov/pictures/) and the Library's "American Memory" website (http://memory.loc.gov/). Researchers interested in a courthouse, post office, or other building in which the federal courts met can search these sites by keyword to locate photographs, data pages, and architectural drawings.

Researchers interested in further background information on the HABS program can visit the related websites of the Library of Congress (http://memory.loc.gov/ammem/collections/habs_haer/) and the National Park Service (http://www.nps.gov/history/hdp/). The administrative records of the HABS program are available in Record Group 515 at the National Archives at College Park, Maryland.

## B. *National Register of Historic Places*

In 1966, Congress authorized the Secretary of the Interior to "expand and maintain a national register of districts, sites, buildings, structures, and objects significant in American history, architecture, archeology, and culture." The National Register of Historic Places maintains an archive of nominations, photographs, correspondence, maps, and blueprints related to buildings and sites that have been nominated for the National Register.

Nomination forms and correspondence describe the historical and architectural significance of the buildings and sites. Information in nomination files includes the various historic names and uses of each building, its address and owner, descriptions of its current and historical physical appearances, and details about significant events that transpired at the site. Nomination forms also include bibliographies of primary and secondary sources that can direct researchers toward other materials that can assist them in their research.

The National Register is in the process of digitizing much of its holdings. Researchers can search for information and images related to particular courthouses at http://nrhp.focus.nps.gov/.

Researchers interested in using the National Register's archive in Washington, D.C., must first make an appointment by calling 202-354-2226. Further information about the archive is available at the National Register's website (http://www.nps.gov/nr/).

Several publications offer historical and architectural information on federal courthouses and other public buildings. In 1901, the Department of the Treasury published *A History of Public Buildings under the Control of the Treasury Department* (Washington, D.C.: G.P.O., 1901), which includes photographs and historical descriptions of more than 300 public buildings, including courthouses, customhouses, post offices, federal office buildings, and other types of facilities. The description for each building includes information relating to appropriations and construction dates, as well as details regarding which departments of the government occupied the various rooms of the building. The images in the *History of Public Buildings* are drawn from the collections of the Public Building Service in Record Group 121 at the National Archives at College Park, Maryland.

Between 1867 and 1920, the Supervising Architect published an annual report that provided information on each public building under control of the Supervising Architect's Office, including completed buildings, projects in the middle of construction, and buildings that had been authorized by Congress but for which work had not yet begun. The annual reports list the name of each building, when land was purchased or acquired through donation, any statutes or appropriations related to the building, whether the building was ever leased or rented, the date the building was occupied, the names of contractors, and other miscellaneous information. A few of the earlier volumes also detail when construction was begun and completed.

Several of the reports include architectural drawings of selected buildings. These renderings often differ substantially in appearance from the completed buildings. Renderings for some buildings also appear in multiple reports, revealing how designs for buildings sometimes changed over time, which was most often the case upon the accession of a new Supervising Architect. Most of the drawings show exterior views, although a few renderings of courtrooms were printed in the 1895 report (published in 1896). Many of the drawings also include small sketches of the floor plan of the building, showing courtrooms, jury rooms, and judges' chambers.

The most useful report for finding general information about pre-1920 federal buildings is the *Annual Report of the Supervising Architect of the Treasury Department for the Fiscal Year Ended June 30[,] 1920* (Washington, D.C.: G.P.O., 1920). This volume includes a 461-page table that lists each public building, alphabetically by city, with most of the previously mentioned historical and architectural information.

The annual reports of the heads of the Treasury, Interior, and Justice Departments for the periods during which those departments oversaw the administration of the federal courts (see Part III) give details regarding the appropriations and expenses of the federal judiciary, including some information about the rental of court space and the construction of public buildings. In the nineteenth century, these reports were published as pamphlets or books, and also as documents in the *United States Congressional Serial Set*. The annual reports of the Secretary of the Treasury also contained the annual report of the Supervising Architect.

Researchers interested in locating congressional statutes related to the construction of historic federal courthouses should first consult the annual reports of the Supervising Architect (1867–1920) and the Treasury Department's *History of Public Buildings* (1901). These volumes list each of the statutes and appropriations related to individual buildings and give a brief description of the purpose of each statute. Researchers can then locate the original legislation in the *United States Statutes at Large*. Congressional legislation may pertain to multiple federal buildings, but Congress also often passed laws related to individual buildings.

# Chapter 15. Images of Federal Courthouses

Researchers interested in locating images of federal courthouses should first consult the Federal Judicial Center's online collection of about 600 images of historic courthouses. The collection is available at the Center's website (http://www.fjc.gov/). Researchers can browse by state and then city to locate selected images of various historic courthouses, as well as a brief historical description of each building's construction and use. The photographs in this collection derive from a number of sources, including the National Archives, the Library of Congress, the General Services Administration, the Department of the Interior, and a few published sources.

## A. National Archives and Records Administration

Most of the images included in the Federal Judicial Center's database were gathered from Record Group 121 (Records of the Public Buildings Service) at the National Archives at College Park, Maryland. The photographs in RG 121 are organized into series, five of which have particularly rich holdings of photographs of federal buildings and courthouses.

- RG 121-BA. Photographs of Federal and Other Buildings, 1857–1942 (24 boxes)
- RG 121-BCP. Photographs of Construction of Federal Buildings, 1885–1954 (157 boxes)
- RG 121-BS. Completion Photographs of Federal Buildings, 1900–1967 (107 boxes)
- RG 121-C. Construction of Post Offices, Custom Houses, and Courthouses, 1876–1939 (40 boxes)
- RG 121-M. Miscellaneous Public Buildings, 1870–1894 (9 boxes)

Of these five series, RG 121-BCP offers the most complete photographic record of the construction and remodeling of federal courthouses. The series includes multiple photographs of many individual buildings, including images of construction sites prior to the beginning of the projects, photographs that document each stage of construction or alteration, and completion photographs of the front and back of each building.

Record Group 121 includes other series that may also be of interest to researchers studying federal courthouses. These include:

- RG 121-A. Photographs of Architectural Ornamentation, 1928–1936 (1 box)
- RG 121-CA. Construction Photographs of the U.S. Court of Appeals and Post Office in San Francisco, California, 1901–1909 (1 box)
- RG 121-CMS. Completed Murals and Sculptures in United States Post Offices and Other Federal Buildings, 1935–1943 (8 boxes)
- RG 121-FES. Sketches Submitted in the "48 States Competition" for Murals to be Placed in Post Offices, 1939 (10 boxes)
- RG 121-GA. Paintings and Sculptures Commissioned by the Section of Fine Arts, 1934–1943 (65 boxes)
- RG 121-LSA. Glass Lantern Slides: Paintings, Murals and Sculptures, 1933–1943 (7 boxes)
- RG 121-LSB. Glass Lantern Slides: Buildings in the United States and Other Countries, 1927–1936 (6 boxes)
- RG 121-MS. Prints and Negatives: Murals, Paintings, and Sculptures in Competitions Sponsored by the Section of Fine Arts, 1934–1943 (113 boxes)
- RG 121-PST. Negatives: Paintings and Sculptures Commissioned by the Section of Fine Arts, 1934–1943 (70 boxes)
- RG 121-PWAP-PWD. Public Works of Art Project, 1933–1934 (42 boxes)
- RG 121-SB. Photographs of Post Office Building Sites, 1900–1939 (5 boxes)

Researchers can access photographs from Record Group 121, as well as photographs in other record groups, at the Still Pictures Reference Room at the National Archives at College Park, Maryland.

Other record groups at the National Archives at College Park, Maryland, may also have images that will be of interest to those researching federal court meeting sites. The General Records of the Federal Works Agency in Record Group 162 include a series of photographs that illustrate the activities of the Public Building Administration, from 1939 to 1943 (RG 162-PBA). These photographs show construction and completion photographs of several buildings that served as courthouses (including post office buildings). The Records of the Post Office Department in Record Group 28 include photographs of postal facilities from 1931 to 1959 (RG 28-F). Some of these photographs, which are organized by state and then by city, show federal buildings that served as both post offices and courthouses. This series includes interior and exterior views of the buildings, although the interior images only show the postal facilities.

## B. Library of Congress

The collections of the Prints and Photographs Division at the Library of Congress include many images of federal buildings and courthouses, some of which can be found online. Researchers can locate digital images of public buildings by executing a keyword search of the Prints and Photographs Division's online catalog (http://www.loc.gov/pictures/) or the Library's "American Memory" website (http://memory.loc.gov/). These websites also provide access to the photographs and drawings that have been digitized from the Historic American Buildings Survey (HABS) reports (see Chapter 14).

In addition to using the online catalog, researchers at the Library of Congress can search the card catalog and vertical files in the Prints and Photographs Division's reading room for other images that have not yet been digitized, including stereoviews (three dimensional photographs, ca. 1860–1920), postcards, 8x10 black and white glossy prints, and large architectural drawings from the Office of the Supervising Architect (ca. 1856–1874). Original copies of the HABS reports are also available in the open stacks of the Prints and Photographs Division's reading room.

## C. National Register of Historic Places

The nomination files in the National Register of Historic Places archive often include photographs of the interior and exterior of the historic buildings at a site. The National Register is in the process of digitizing the nomination files in its collection. Researchers can search http://nrhp.focus.nps.gov/ for digitized records and images related to particular courthouses.

Researchers interested in using the archive of the National Register in Washington, D.C., must first make an appointment by calling 202-354-2226. Further information about the archive is available at the National Register's website (http://www.nps.gov/nr/).

## D.  Center for Historic Buildings

The General Services Administration (GSA) maintains the Center for Historic Buildings to provide "technical and strategic expertise to promote the viability, reuse, and integrity of historic buildings GSA owns, leases, and has the opportunity to acquire." The GSA maintains a "Historic Federal Building Database" at its website (http://www.gsa.gov/), through which researchers can search for photographs, as well as historical and architectural information related to the buildings that the GSA owns or leases.

## E.  Local Repositories

Many local and regional archival repositories maintain photographic archives that include images of federal courthouses. Researchers interested in locating images of local court meeting places should contact historical societies, public libraries, universities, newspapers, county archives, state archives, and state historical commissions to determine whether their photographic collections have any photographic records of interest.

# Part V. Research Collections

# Chapter 16. Personal Records

## A. Introduction

To further their research, researchers in federal judicial history can use the personal papers of judges, court personnel, members of Congress, executive branch officers, lawyers, journalists, and parties in court cases. Collections of personal papers complement the official government records held by the National Archives and Records Administration. As noted in Parts I and III, only a few private manuscript collections are held by the National Archives. Most personal research collections available to researchers are maintained by libraries and archival repositories throughout the United States.

The following sections describe some of the types of collections that researchers in federal judicial history may wish to consult.

## B. Federal Judges

The personal manuscript collections of federal judges often include private correspondence, diaries, journals, newspaper clippings files, speeches, awards, invitations, photographs, and other assorted materials. Many manuscript collections also include the judge's chambers papers, such as the judge's notes on oral arguments, memorandums sent to or received from law clerks, bench memorandums, voting memorandums, correspondence with other judges, draft opinions and orders, opinion galleys with handwritten revisions, slip opinions, correspondence with the public, conference notes, scrapbooks, and other assorted papers. Recent "manuscript" collections may also include electronic files, such as emails, digital photographs, audio and video recordings, and word-processing files.

The Federal Judicial History Office maintains within the Biographical Directory of Federal Judges information related to research collections of judges, as well to the manuscript collections of persons with whom federal judges corresponded. Researchers can locate relevant archival material by searching for particular judges in the Biographical Directory of Federal Judges at http://www.fjc.gov/ and by selecting the link for "Research Collections," which is located at the bottom of the biography of each judge for whom a collection is available.

Published editions of judges' personal papers can be an easily accessible and useful resource for the history of a particular judge or court. In some cases, judges' papers have been published as a book or series of volumes; other judges' collections have been excerpted or abridged and published as articles in historical journals and magazines. Researchers can access bibliographic information for published primary sources related to federal judges by selecting the "Bibliography" link at the bottom of a judge's biography in the Biographical Directory of Federal Judges. The Bibliography link directs researchers to available secondary sources related to the judge.

The Biographical Directory of Federal Judges also directs researchers to oral histories that have been conducted with federal judges. Oral histories may include an audio or video recording as well as an edited transcript.

## C. Court Officers

The private papers of U.S. attorneys, marshals, clerks of court, and other court officers can be useful when writing about the history of the federal judiciary. As noted in Chapter 12, many of the early U.S. marshals and U.S. attorneys retained their official papers as personal property at the end of their terms of service. As a consequence, manuscript collections of court officers may be composed of both personal papers and official records. The personal research collections of court officers may include personal papers, such as private correspondence, journals and diaries, newspaper clippings, photographs, and scrapbooks, as well as official records, such as case papers, dockets, financial records, warrants, ledgers, and official correspondence.

Most manuscript collections of court officers that are available for public research are held in private repositories and can be located by searching archival research databases (described below). In a few rare instances, the personal papers of court officers were transferred to the National Archives along with the official records of the U.S. district and circuit courts they served (see Chapter 1).

## D. Supreme Court Reporters

The papers of the early Supreme Court reporters are readily available and may offer some insight into the functions of the Court. The Historical Society of Pennsylvania, in Philadelphia, holds the family papers of both Alexander J. Dallas and Richard Peters, Jr. Temple University also has a large collection of Dallas's correspondence. Benjamin Chew Howard's family papers are held at the Maryland Historical Society, in Baltimore. The Jeremiah S. Black Papers, at the Library of Congress, have been microfilmed and are available through Interlibrary Loan (microfilm reels 17–20 cover the years 1861 and 1862, when Black served as reporter for the Court). The papers of Henry Wheaton and John William Wallace are held by their alma mater, Brown University. The research collections of the Court's second reporter, William Cranch, who also served as a judge on the Circuit Court of the District of Columbia, are listed under his biography in the Biographical Directory of Federal Judges at http://www.fjc.gov/.

## E. Members of Congress

The manuscript collections of members of Congress may provide insight into the relationship between the legislative and judicial branches of the federal government, particularly as Congress shaped legislation related to the judiciary and as senators considered judicial nominations. The personal papers of members of Congress often include correspondence with or about federal judges. Constituents also frequently corresponded with their senators and representatives regarding the organization and jurisdiction of the federal courts, the need for additional judgeships or judicial districts, and pending judicial nominations. Researchers can locate congressional papers through the Congressional Biographical Directory, which is available online at http://bioguide.congress.gov/.

## F. Presidents and Executive Branch Officials

The manuscript collections of Presidents and Cabinet members often include correspondence with and about members of the federal judiciary. The personal papers of the early Presidents, Attorneys General, and Secretaries of State also often include papers and correspondence related to presidential nominations, as well as correspondence regarding litigation in the federal courts or needed reforms in the judicial system.

Much of the personal and official correspondence of the early Presidents and executive branch officers has been published in documentary editions, many of which draw from both personal manuscript collections and official government records at the National Archives. In recent years, several presidential manuscript collections have also been digitized and made available on the Internet. Researchers can use these published and digitized collections to locate information about judicial nominations and appointments, proposed legislation affecting the judiciary, and the personal interactions between members of the judiciary and the executive branch of the federal government.

The National Archives and Records Administration maintains presidential libraries for every President since Herbert Hoover. Presidential libraries house the presidential papers of the Presidents and their administrations as well as the personal research collections of the Presidents and some of their associates. Researchers can access archival and electronic materials at presidential libraries subject to the provisions of the Freedom of Information Act (FOIA). The National Archives and the presidential libraries have also placed a number of historical documents, finding aids, and other resources online. Links to the websites of the presidential libraries are available at http://www.archives.gov/presidential-libraries/.

Several archival repositories patterned after the presidential libraries have been established for pre-Hoover Presidents, including Abraham Lincoln and Rutherford B. Hayes. Many early presidential research collections are housed at the Library of Congress, as well as at numerous other libraries and archival repositories. As noted in Chapter 12, the official papers of the early Attorneys General were often retained as personal property at the end of each presidential administration and may be included with the Attorneys General's personal papers at archival repositories outside of the National Archives.

## G. A Note on the Papers of Lawyers and Law Firms

The private papers of attorneys and law firms can sometimes be used for historical research, but these papers may be restricted because of attorney–client privilege. Attorney–client privilege protects confidential communications between lawyers and their clients from being disclosed until consent for release has been given by the client. Lawyers' papers that have been donated to a library or archive may have restricted access because of this privilege. Some libraries open such records to researchers after each person involved in the attorney–client relationship is deceased, or after a set period of time. Other lawyers' files have been closed to researchers for more than a century because the client never granted permission to have them opened (and the client had no heirs who could grant that permission). Researchers who locate papers held by libraries or archives, law firms, or the lawyers themselves must be aware that some lawyers' papers may be privileged and confidential, and as a consequence unavailable for research and publication.

## H. Locating Archival Resources

Researchers can use a number of resources to locate the personal research collections of federal judges and other persons who have impacted the federal judiciary. Since 1959, the Library of Congress has cataloged archival collections in the United States in the *National Union Catalog of Manuscript Collections* (NUCMC). Several subscription databases, including ArchivesUSA (http://archives.chadwyck.com/) and FirstSearch (http://www.oclc.org/), allow researchers to search the listings in NUCMC by title, keyword, or subject heading. The Library of Congress provides free access to the NUCMC listings on FirstSearch through the Library's website (http://www.loc.gov/coll/nucmc/index.html).

Other websites and books can also be useful for locating archival collections related to the federal judiciary. The American Historical Association recently created an "Archives Wiki" that allows researchers to search for information about archival repositories around the world (http://archiveswiki.historians.org/). The National Historical Publications and Records Commission has compiled a thorough list of archival repositories in its *Directory of Archives and Manuscript Repositories in the United States*, second edition (Phoenix: Oryx Press, 1988).

## I. Finding Aids

Most libraries and archival repositories prepare finding aids to help make their collections accessible to researchers. The content and shape of these research tools varies widely from institution to institution. Some libraries create finding aids that describe the libraries' collections down to the box, folder, or item level. Other libraries provide only general descriptions of their collections.

Libraries are increasingly putting their finding aids online so that researchers can locate relevant archival collections prior to visiting the archive. If such information is not available through a repository's website, researchers can contact the library to find out whether finding aids have been prepared for the particular collections they wish to use.

# Appendices

Appendix A. Resources Available Through the Federal Judicial History Office

Appendix B. Preliminary Inventories and Finding Aids for Judiciary-Related Records at the National Archives

Appendix C. Court Records at the National Archives (by record group)

Appendix D. Locations of Federal Court Records at the National Archives (by state or by type of court)

Appendix E. National Archives Locations

Appendix F. Court Records Held Outside of the National Archives

# Appendix A. Resources Available Through the Federal Judicial History Office

The Federal Judicial History Office has created a number of resources that will be of use to researchers interested in federal judicial history. All of these resources are available through the "History of the Federal Judiciary" section of the Federal Judicial Center's website (http://www.fjc. gov/). Each of the following subheadings describes the resources available at a particular section of the History of the Federal Judiciary site. Researchers can contact the Federal Judicial History Office by phone at 202-502-4180, or by email at history@fjc.gov.

## Judges of the United States Courts

The Federal Judicial History Office has compiled and maintains a biographical directory of all life-tenured judges who have served on the federal bench from 1789 to the present. Each directory listing includes the judge's birth and death dates, places of birth and death, educational background, professional career, nomination and confirmation dates, and service on the federal bench. Where available, the directory lists manuscript collections that contain correspondence of the judge, a bibliography of secondary works about the judge, a listing of oral history interviews given by the judge, links to websites devoted to the judge's career, and information on portraits or photographs of the judge. Researchers can search the directory by name, court, court type, nominating President, party of nominating President, nomination date, confirmation date, commission date, senior status date, termination date, reason for termination, race or ethnicity, and gender. Researchers can also limit their queries to sitting judges or judges for whom the directory lists reference sources.

The section of the website on judges also includes historical information on bankruptcy and magistrate judgeships, judicial salaries, impeachments, and milestones of judicial service.

## Courts of the Federal Judiciary

The History Office's website provides researchers with a brief historical sketch of each type of federal court, a listing of congressional legislation related to individual courts, a list of judges who served on the court, a list of the cities in which the court met, a bibliography of books and articles about the court, and a listing of which National Archives facilities hold the court's official records.

## Teaching Judicial History: Notable Federal Trials

The Federal Judicial History Office has compiled a series of teaching units on notable federal trials. The stories of historic federal trials offer an opportunity to explore the role of the judiciary in the public life of the nation. The Federal Judicial Center developed this educational program to provide educators and students with accessible information about the history of the federal courts and to facilitate the use of court-related materials in classrooms.

Each unit in the program focuses on a notable case that reflects important topics examined in history and government courses at the high school and college levels. Each unit includes extensive background on the case and related historical documents. Curriculum strategies allow teachers to incorporate the unit materials in their courses and provide suggestions for judges that support the use of historical materials in civic education outreach.

## Talking Points on Judicial History

The Federal Judicial History Office has assembled a series of talking points on several important aspects of judicial history, including the constitutional origins of the federal courts, judicial independence, and the establishment of the federal judiciary. Each unit also includes discussion questions, primary historical documents, a bibliography, and a PowerPoint™ presentation.

## Historic Federal Courthouses

The Federal Judicial Center has compiled and presented online nearly 600 images of historic federal courthouses and other meeting places of federal courts. Researchers can browse by state and then city to locate selected images of various historic courthouses as well as a brief historical sketch of each building. The photographs online derive from a number of sources, including the National Archives, the Library of Congress, the General Services Administration, the Department of the Interior, and a few published sources. Courthouse images on the Center's website are in the public domain and can be downloaded and reproduced free of charge. Researchers interested in locating additional images of court meeting places should consult Part IV of this guide.

## Judicial Administration

The Federal Judicial Center's "History of the Federal Judiciary" website provides historical information about the administration of the federal courts since their establishment in 1789. The site includes brief descriptions of types of officers and staff who have worked in the federal courts, as well as descriptions of the Office of the Chief Justice, the Judicial Conference of the United States, the Administrative Office of the United States Courts, the Federal Judicial Center, the U.S. Sentencing Commission, and the executive branch departments that were responsible for the administration of the federal judiciary prior to the creation of the Administrative Office in 1939. In addition, the site lists the directors of the Administrative Office, the directors and Board members of the Federal Judicial Center, the members of the Judicial Conference, and the chairs of the judiciary committees in the House of Representatives and Senate from 1813 and 1816, respectively, to the present. This section of the website also includes brief histories (with citations to relevant statutes) related to the organization of the judicial circuits.

## Landmark Judicial Legislation

This section of the Center's website provides researchers with a historical sketch and the text (or an excerpt from the text) of legislation that affected the size, scope, organization, or administration of the federal judiciary, beginning with Article III of the U.S. Constitution (1787) and the Judiciary Act of 1789. Researchers interested in legislation related to individual courts can locate citations to that legislation under the "Courts of the Federal Judiciary" section of the website.

## Federal Court Historical Programs

This section of the Federal Judicial Center's website provides researchers with links to the websites of federal court history programs, sites, and societies. It also includes a bibliography of recently published histories of federal courts.

Persons interested in starting a court historical program can download a PDF version of *Initiating a Court Historical Program* (Washington,

D.C.: Federal Judicial Center, 2004). This section of the website also provides resources and information for persons interested in conducting oral history interviews.

## Publications

The following is a list of recent publications by the Federal Judicial History Office. Researchers can download PDF versions of Federal Judicial Center publications from the Center's website (http://www.fjc.gov/).

*A Guide to the Preservation of Federal Judges' Papers*, 2nd edition. Washington, D.C.: Federal Judicial Center, 2009.

*Initiating a Court Historical Program*. Washington, D.C.: Federal Judicial Center, 2004.

Messinger, I. Scott. *Order in the Courts: A History of the Federal Court Clerk's Office*. Washington, D.C.: Federal Judicial Center, 2002.

Wheeler, Russell R., and Cynthia Harrison. *Creating the Federal Judicial System*, 3rd edition. Washington, D.C.: Federal Judicial Center, 2005.

# Appendix B. Preliminary Inventories and Finding Aids for Judiciary-Related Records at the National Archives

The National Archives and Records Administration has created preliminary inventories and finding aids for many of its holdings. Many of these inventories have been published and are available at libraries outside of the National Archives system. Others—including most of the inventories for the records of the federal courts in Record Groups 21, 276, and 527—are unpublished documents that are only available onsite at the branch of the National Archives where the records are held. Older preliminary inventories may not accurately reflect the current scope and organization of a record group. Still, they can be a useful tool for determining the types of materials included in a collection.

At various times, private companies and universities have microfilmed records held at the National Archives. Many of these microfilm editions include finding aids that are useful for accessing the original records at the National Archives. Several federal departments and agencies have also created finding aids for their official records.

The following bibliography lists preliminary inventories and finding aids that have been created by the National Archives, by other federal departments or agencies, and by nongovernmental organizations. The materials listed in this appendix do not include the pamphlets or other prefatory materials that accompany NARA microfilm that are described in this guide's Introduction.

## Congress

Coren, Robert W., Mary Rephlo, David Kepley, and Charles South, comps. *Guide to the Records of the United States Senate at the National Archives, 1789–1989: Bicentennial Edition.* Washington, D.C.: U.S. Senate, 1989.

Hufford, Harold E., and Watson G. Caudill, comps. *Preliminary Inventory of the Records of the United States Senate.* Washington, D.C.: National Archives, 1950.

Perros, George P., James C. Brown, and Jacqueline A. Wood, comps. *Papers of the United States Senate Relating to Presidential Nominations, 1789–1901*. Washington, D.C.: National Archives and Records Service, 1964.

Rowland, Buford, Handy B. Fant, and Harold E. Huford, comps. *Preliminary Inventory of the Records of the United States House of Representatives, 1789–1946*. 2 vols. Washington, D.C.: National Archives and Records Service, 1959.

Rowland, Buford, Jose D. Lizardo, and George P. Perros, comps. *Printed Hearings of the House of Representatives Found Among Its Committee Records in the National Archives of the United States, 1824–1958*. Washington, D.C.: National Archives and Records Service, 1974.

Schamel, Charles E., Mary Rephlo, Rodney Ross, David Kepley, Robert W. Coren, and James Gregory Bradsher, comps. *Guide to the Records of the United States House of Representatives at the National Archives, 1789–1989: Bicentennial Edition*. Washington, D.C.: U.S. House of Representatives, 1989.

## Department of State

Department of State. *Calendar of the Correspondence of James Madison*. Washington, D.C.: Department of State, 1894.

_____. *Calendar of the Correspondence of Thomas Jefferson*. 3 vols. Washington, D.C.: Department of State, 1894–1903.

_____. *Calendar of the Miscellaneous Letters Received by the Department of State, from the Organization of the Government to 1820*. Washington, D.C.: G.P.O., 1897.

Hunt, Gaillard, comp. *Calendar of Applications and Recommendations for Office during the Presidency of George Washington, Prepared from the Files of the Bureau of Appointments, Department of State*. Washington, D.C.: G.P.O., 1901.

Staff of the Diplomatic Branch, Department of State, comps. *Inventory of the General Records of the Department of State: Record Group 59*, microfilm ed. Washington, D.C.: National Archives and Records Administration, 1992.

*Guide to Research in Federal Judicial History*

## Department of the Interior

Hill, Edward E., and Renee Jaussaud, comps. *Inventory of the Records of the Department of the Interior: Record Group 48*. Washington, D.C.: National Archives and Records Administration, 1987.

Rowland, Catherine M., comp. *Index to Appropriation Ledgers in the Records of the Office of the Secretary of the Interior, Division of Finance, 1853–1923 (Record Group 48)*. Washington, D.C.: National Archives and Records Service, 1963.

## Department of Justice

Johnson, Marion M., comp. *Preliminary Inventory of the General Records of the Department of Justice: Record Group 60*. Washington, D.C.: National Archives and Records Service, 1981.

Johnson, Marion M., comp. *Preliminary Inventory of the Records of the United States Attorneys and Marshals (Record Group 118)*. Washington, D.C.: National Archives and Records Service, 1964.

Kerner, Gaiselle, comp. *Preliminary Inventory of the Office of the Pardon Attorney (Record Group 204)*. Washington, D.C.: National Archives and Records Service, 1955.

Lester, Robert E., comp. *A Guide to the Microfilm Edition of Federal Bureau of Investigation Confidential Files: The U.S. Supreme Court and Federal Judges Subject Files*. Bethesda, Md.: Univesity Publications of America, 1991.

Lewis, Daniel, comp. *Letters Received by the Attorney General, 1809–1870: Southern Law and Order*. Bethesda, Md.: LexisNexis, 2001.

Schipper, Martin, comp. *Letters Received by the Attorney General, 1809–1870: Western Law and Order*. Bethesda, Md.: LexisNexis, 1996.

_____. *Letters Received by the Attorney General, 1871–1884: Western Law and Order*. Bethesda, Md.: LexisNexis, 2003.

Short, Justin Owen, and Alice Chen, comp. *Letters Received by the Attorney General, 1871–1884: Southern Law and Order*. Bethesda, Md.: LexisNexis, 2005.

Taynor, Kristen M., comp. *Letters Received by the Attorney General, 1809–1870: Federal Government Correspondence.* Bethesda, Md.: LexisNexis, 2007.

————. *Letters Received by the Attorney General, 1809–1870: Northern Law and Order.* Bethesda, Md.: LexisNexis, 2003.

## Department of the Treasury

Holverstott, Lyle J., comp. *Preliminary Inventory of the Records of the United States Secret Service.* Washington, D.C.: National Archives, 1949.

King, Donald L., and William F. Sherman, comps. *Preliminary Inventory of the Records of the Bureau of Accounts (Treasury) (Record Group 39).* Washington, D.C.: National Archives and Records Service, 1963.

Ryan, Carmelita S., and Hope K. Holdcamper, comps. *Preliminary Inventory of the General Records of the Department of the Treasury: Record Group 56.* Washington, D.C., National Archives and Records Service, 1977.

Sherman, William F., and Craig R. Scott, comps. *Records of the Accounting Officers of the Department of the Treasury: Inventory 14 (Revised).* Lovettsville, Va.: Willow Bend Books, 1997.

Ulibarri, George S., comp. *Preliminary Inventory of the Records of the Solicitor of the Treasury (Record Group 206).* Washington, D.C.: National Archives and Records Service, 1968.

Van Neste, W. Lane, and Virgil E. Baugh, comps. *Preliminary Inventory of the Records of the Public Buildings Service.* Washington, D.C.: National Archives and Records Service, 1958.

## Federal Courts

Allen, Hardee, and Janet Weiner, comps. *Preliminary Inventory of the Records of the United States Commerce Court.* Washington, D.C.: National Archives and Records Service, 1962.

Johnson, Marion M., comp. *Preliminary Inventory of the Records of the Supreme Court of the United States.* Washington, D.C.: National Archives and Records Service, 1962, rev. ed., 1973, microfilm supplement, 1985.

Johnson, Marion M., Elaine C. Everly, and Toussaint L. Prince, comps. *Index to the Manuscript and Revised Printed Opinions of the Supreme Court of the United States in the National Archives, 1808–73*. Washington, D.C.: National Archives and Records Service, 1965.

Johnson, Marion M., Mary Jo Grotenrath, and Henry T. Ulasek, comps. *Preliminary Inventory of the Records of the United States District Court for the Eastern District of Pennsylvania (Record Group 21)*. Washington, D.C.: National Archives and Records Service, 1960.

Kerner, Gaiselle, comp. *Preliminary Inventory of the Records of the United States Court of Claims*. Washington, D.C.: National Archives and Records Service, 1953.

National Archives and Records Administration. *Federal Court Records: A Select Catalog of National Archives Microfilm Publications*. Washington, D.C.: National Archives and Records Administration, 1987.

Robinton, Madeline Russell. *An Introduction to the Papers of the New York Prize Court, 1861–1865*. New York: Columbia University Press, 1945.

Ulasek, Henry T., and Marion Johnson, comps. *Preliminary Inventory of the Records of the United States District Court for the Southern District of New York (Record Group 21)*. Washington, D.C.: National Archives and Records Service, 1959.

Weinert, Janet, comp. *Preliminary Inventory of the Records of the United States District Court for the District of Columbia*. Washington, D.C.: National Archives and Records Service, 1964.

# Appendix C. Court Records at the National Archives (by record group)

Record Group 21:    Records of District Courts [and Circuit Courts] of the United States

Record Group 116:   Records of the Administrative Office of the United States Courts

Record Group 123:   Records of the United States Court of Claims

Record Group 172:   Records of the United States Commerce Court

Record Group 267:   Records of the Supreme Court of the United States

Record Group 276:   Records of the United States Courts of Appeals

Record Group 308:   Records of the U.S. Tax Court

Record Group 321:   Records of the U.S. Court of International Trade

Record Group 477:   Records of the U.S. Foreign Intelligence Surveillance Court

Record Group 482:   Records of the Judicial Panel on Multidistrict Litigation

Record Group 502:   Records of the U.S. Court of Federal Claims

Record Group 503:   Records of the U.S. Court of Customs and Patent Appeals

Record Group 504:   Records of the U.S. Court of Appeals for the Federal Circuit

Record Group 516:   Records of the Federal Judicial Center

Record Group 521:   Records of the U.S. Court of Appeals for Veterans Claims

Record Group 539:   Records of the United States Sentencing Commission

Record Group 578:   Records of the United States Bankruptcy Courts

# Appendix D. Locations of Federal Court Records at the National Archives (by state or by type of court)

## Supreme Court of the United States

The records of the Supreme Court of the United States are held in Record Group 267 at the National Archives in Washington, D.C. Nontextual records are held at the National Archives at College Park, Maryland.

## U.S. Courts of Appeals

### U.S. Court of Appeals for the First Circuit

The records of the U.S. Court of Appeals for the First Circuit are included among Record Group 276 at the National Archives at Boston.

### U.S. Court of Appeals for the Second Circuit

The records of the U.S. Court of Appeals for the Second Circuit are included among Record Group 276 at the National Archives at New York City.

### U.S. Court of Appeals for the Third Circuit

The records of the U.S. Court of Appeals for the Third Circuit are included among Record Group 276 at the National Archives at Philadelphia.

### U.S. Court of Appeals for the Fourth Circuit

The records of the U.S. Court of Appeals for the Fourth Circuit are included among Record Group 276 at the National Archives at Philadelphia.

### U.S. Court of Appeals for the Fifth Circuit

The records of the U.S. Court of Appeals for the Fifth Circuit are included among Record Group 276 at the National Archives at Fort Worth.

## U.S. Court of Appeals for the Sixth Circuit

The records of the U.S. Court of Appeals for the Sixth Circuit are included among Record Group 276 at the National Archives at Chicago.

## U.S. Court of Appeals for the Seventh Circuit

The records of the U.S. Court of Appeals for the Seventh Circuit are included among Record Group 276 at the National Archives at Chicago.

## U.S. Court of Appeals for the Eighth Circuit

The records of the U.S. Court of Appeals for the Eighth Circuit are included among Record Group 276 at the National Archives at Kansas City.

## U.S. Court of Appeals for the Ninth Circuit

The records of the U.S. Court of Appeals for the Ninth Circuit are included among Record Group 276 at the National Archives at San Francisco.

## U.S. Court of Appeals for the Tenth Circuit

The records of the U.S. Court of Appeals for the Tenth Circuit are included among Record Group 276 at the National Archives at Denver.

## U.S. Court of Appeals for the Eleventh Circuit

The records of the U.S. Court of Appeals for the Eleventh Circuit are included among Record Group 276 at the National Archives at Atlanta.

## U.S. Court of Appeals for the District of Columbia Circuit

The records of the U.S. Court of Appeals for the District of Columbia Circuit are included among Record Group 276 at the National Archives in Washington, D.C.

## U.S. Court of Appeals for the Federal Circuit

The records of the U.S. Court of Appeals for the Federal Circuit have not yet been accessioned by the National Archives and Records Administration. Once accessioned, these records will make up Record Group 504 at the National Archives in Washington, D.C.

## U.S. District and Circuit Courts (by state)

### Alabama

The records of the U.S. District Courts and U.S. Circuit Courts for the judicial districts of Alabama are included among Record Group 21 at the National Archives at Atlanta.

### Alaska

The records of the U.S. District Court for the District of Alaska are included among Record Group 21 at the National Archives at Anchorage.

### Arizona

The records of the U.S. District Court for the District of Arizona are included among Record Group 21 at the National Archives at Riverside.

### Arkansas

The records of the U.S. District Courts and U.S. Circuit Courts for the judicial districts of Arkansas are included among Record Group 21 at the National Archives at Fort Worth.

### California

The records of the U.S. District Court for the Northern District of California, 1850–1866, and 1886 to the present, are included among Record Group 21 at the National Archives at San Francisco.

The general records of the U.S. District Court for the Southern District of California, 1850–1866, are included among Record Group 21 at the National Archives at Riverside. The case records of the U.S. District Court for the Southern District of California, 1850–1866, are included among Record Group 21 at the National Archives at San Francisco. The records of the U.S. District Court for the Southern District of California, since 1886, are included among Record Group 21 at the National Archives at Riverside, with the exception of the records of the Southern District, Northern Division, 1900–1966, which are included among Record Group 21 at the National Archives at San Francisco.

The records of the U.S. Circuit Court for the California Circuit, 1855–1863, are included among Record Group 21 at the National Archives at San Francisco.

The records of the U.S. Circuit Courts for the Northern and Southern Districts of California, 1863–1866, are included among Record Group 21 at the National Archives at San Francisco.

The records of the U.S. District Court and U.S. Circuit Court for the District of California, 1866–1886, are included among Record Group 21 at the National Archives at San Francisco.

The records of the U.S. Circuit Court for the Northern District of California, 1886–1911, are included among Record Group 21 at the National Archives at San Francisco.

The records of the U.S. Circuit Court for the Southern District of California, 1886–1911, are included among Record Group 21 at the National Archives at Riverside.

The records of the U.S. District Court for the Central District of California are included among Record Group 21 at the National Archives at Riverside.

The records of the U.S. District Court for the Eastern District of California are included among Record Group 21 at the National Archives at San Francisco.

## Colorado
The records of the U.S. District Court and U.S. Circuit Court for the District of Colorado are included among Record Group 21 at the National Archives at Denver.

## Connecticut
The records of the U.S. District Court and U.S. Circuit Court for the District of Connecticut are included among Record Group 21 at the National Archives at Boston.

## Delaware
The records of the U.S. District Court and U.S. Circuit Court for the District of Delaware are included among Record Group 21 at the National Archives at Philadelphia.

## District of Columbia
Minutes of the District Court for the District of Potomac, 1801–1802, are included in Record Group 21 at the National Archives in Wash-

ington, D.C., as well as among the records of Arlington County at the Library of Virginia, in Richmond.

The records of the Washington County term of the U.S. Circuit Court of the District of Columbia are included among Record Group 21 at the National Archives in Washington, D.C.

The records of the Alexandria County term of the U.S. Circuit Court of the District of Columbia are held at the Library of Virginia, in Richmond.

The records of the Criminal Court of the District of Columbia are included among Record Group 21 at the National Archives in Washington, D.C.

The records of the Supreme Court of the District of Columbia are included among Record Group 21 at the National Archives in Washington, D.C.

The records of the U.S. District Court for the District of Columbia are included among Record Group 21 at the National Archives in Washington, D.C.

## Florida

The records of the U.S. District Courts and U.S. Circuit Courts for the judicial districts of Florida are included among Record Group 21 at the National Archives at Atlanta.

## Georgia

The records of the U.S. District Courts and U.S. Circuit Courts for the judicial districts of Georgia are included among Record Group 21 at the National Archives at Atlanta.

## Hawaii

The records of the U.S. District Court for the District of Hawaii are included among Record Group 21 at the National Archives at San Francisco.

## Idaho

The records of the U.S. District Court and U.S. Circuit Court for the District of Idaho are included among Record Group 21 at the National Archives at Seattle.

## Illinois

The records of the U.S. District Courts and U.S. Circuit Courts for the judicial districts of Illinois are included among Record Group 21 at the National Archives at Chicago.

## Indiana

The records of the U.S. District Courts and U.S. Circuit Courts for the judicial districts of Indiana are included among Record Group 21 at the National Archives at Chicago.

## Iowa

The records of the U.S. District Courts and U.S. Circuit Courts for the judicial districts of Iowa are included among Record Group 21 at the National Archives at Kansas City.

## Kansas

The records of the U.S. District Court and U.S. Circuit Court for the District of Kansas are included among Record Group 21 at the National Archives at Kansas City.

## Kentucky

The records of the U.S. District Courts and U.S. Circuit Courts for the judicial districts of Kentucky are included among Record Group 21 at the National Archives at Atlanta.

## Louisiana

The records of the U.S. District Courts and U.S. Circuit Courts for the judicial districts of Louisiana are included among Record Group 21 at the National Archives at Fort Worth.

## Maine

The records of the U.S. District Court and U.S. Circuit Court for the District of Maine are included among Record Group 21 at the National Archives at Boston.

## Maryland

The records of the U.S. District Court and U.S. Circuit Court for the District of Maryland are included among Record Group 21 at the National Archives at Philadelphia.

## Massachusetts

The records of the U.S. District Court and U.S. Circuit Court for the District of Massachusetts are included among Record Group 21 at the National Archives at Boston.

## Michigan

The records of the U.S. District Courts and U.S. Circuit Courts for the judicial districts of Michigan are included among Record Group 21 at the National Archives at Chicago.

## Minnesota

The records of the U.S. District Court and U.S. Circuit Court for the District of Minnesota are included among Record Group 21 at the National Archives at Chicago.

## Mississippi

The records of the U.S. District Courts and U.S. Circuit Courts for the judicial districts of Mississippi are included among Record Group 21 at the National Archives at Atlanta.

## Missouri

The records of the U.S. District Courts and U.S. Circuit Courts for the judicial districts of Missouri are included among Record Group 21 at the National Archives at Kansas City.

## Montana

The records of the U.S. District Court and U.S. Circuit Court for the District of Montana are included among Record Group 21 at the National Archives at Denver.

## Nebraska

The records of the U.S. District Court and U.S. Circuit Court for the District of Nebraska are included among Record Group 21 at the National Archives at Kansas City.

## Nevada

The records of the U.S. District Court and U.S. Circuit Court for the District of Nevada (except for the Las Vegas sessions of the former) are included among Record Group 21 at the National Archives at San Francisco.

The records of the U.S. District Court for the District of Nevada (Las Vegas sessions only) are included among Record Group 21 at the National Archives at Riverside.

## New Hampshire

The records of the U.S. District Court and U.S. Circuit Court for the District of New Hampshire are included among Record Group 21 at the National Archives at Boston.

## New Jersey

The records of the U.S. District Courts and U.S. Circuit Court for the judicial districts of New Jersey are included among Record Group 21 at the National Archives at New York City.

## New Mexico

The records of the U.S. District Court for the District of New Mexico are included among Record Group 21 at the National Archives at Denver.

## New York

The records of the U.S. District Courts and U.S. Circuit Courts for the judicial districts of New York are included among Record Group 21 at the National Archives at New York City.

## North Carolina

The records of the U.S. District Courts and U.S. Circuit Courts for the judicial districts of North Carolina are included among Record Group 21 at the National Archives at Atlanta.

## North Dakota

The records of the U.S. District Court and U.S. Circuit Court for the District of North Dakota are included among Record Group 21 at the National Archives at Denver.

## Ohio

The records of the U.S. District Courts and U.S. Circuit Courts for the judicial districts of Ohio are included among Record Group 21 at the National Archives at Chicago.

## Oklahoma

The records of the U.S. District Courts and U.S. Circuit Courts for the judicial districts of Oklahoma are included among Record Group 21 at the National Archives at Fort Worth.

## Oregon

The records of the U.S. District Court and U.S. Circuit Court for the District of Oregon are included among Record Group 21 at the National Archives at Seattle.

## Pennsylvania

The records of the U.S. District Courts and U.S. Circuit Courts for the judicial districts of Pennsylvania are included among Record Group 21 at the National Archives at Philadelphia.

## Puerto Rico

The records of the U.S. District Court for the District of Puerto Rico are included among Record Group 21 at the National Archives at New York City.

## Rhode Island

The records of the U.S. District Court and U.S. Circuit Court for the District of Rhode Island are included among Record Group 21 at the National Archives at Boston.

## South Carolina

The records of the U.S. District Courts and U.S. Circuit Court for the judicial districts of South Carolina are included among Record Group 21 at the National Archives at Atlanta.

## South Dakota

The records of the U.S. District Court and U.S. Circuit Court for the District of South Dakota are included among Record Group 21 at the National Archives at Denver.

## Tennessee

The records of the U.S. District Courts and U.S. Circuit Courts for the judicial districts of Tennessee are included among Record Group 21 at the National Archives at Atlanta.

## Texas

The records of the U.S. District Courts and U.S. Circuit Courts for the judicial districts of Texas are included among Record Group 21 at the National Archives at Fort Worth.

## Utah

The records of the U.S. District Court and U.S. Circuit Court for the District of Utah are included among Record Group 21 at the National Archives at Denver.

## Vermont

The records of the U.S. District Court and U.S. Circuit Court for the District of Vermont are included among Record Group 21 at the National Archives at Boston.

## Virginia

The records of the U.S. District Courts and U.S. Circuit Courts for the judicial districts of Virginia are included among Record Group 21 at the National Archives at Philadelphia.

## Washington

The records of the U.S. District Courts and U.S. Circuit Courts for the judicial districts of Washington are included among Record Group 21 at the National Archives at Seattle.

## West Virginia

The records of the U.S. District Courts and U.S. Circuit Courts for the judicial districts of West Virginia are included among Record Group 21 at the National Archives at Philadelphia.

## Wisconsin

The records of the U.S. District Courts and U.S. Circuit Courts for the judicial districts of Wisconsin are included among Record Group 21 at the National Archives at Chicago.

## Wyoming

The records of the U.S. District Court and U.S. Circuit Court for the District of Wyoming are included among Record Group 21 at the National Archives at Denver.

## Federal Courts of Special Jurisdiction

### Court of Claims

The records of the Court of Claims are held in Record Group 123 at the National Archives in Washington, D.C.

### U.S. Court of Federal Claims

The records of the U.S. Court of Federal Claims have not yet been accessioned by the National Archives and Records Administration. Once accessioned, these records will make up Record Group 502 at the National Archives in Washington, D.C.

### U.S. Court of International Trade

The records of the U.S. Court of International Trade, and its predecessors, the U.S. Customs Court and the Board of General Appraisers are included among Record Group 321. The records of the Board of General Appraisers and the U.S. Customs Court are held at the National Archives at New York City. The records of the U.S. Court of International Trade are still maintained by the court, pending their accession by the National Archives.

### U.S. Court of Customs and Patent Appeals

The records of the U.S. Court of Customs and Patent Appeals were transferred to the U.S. Court of Appeals for the Federal Circuit in 1982. Some of the court's early records have since been accessioned by the National Archives and Records Administration and are organized as Record Group 503 at the National Archives in Washington, D.C.

### Commerce Court

The records of the Commerce Court are held in Record Group 172 at the National Archives in Washington, D.C.

### Emergency Court of Appeals
### Temporary Emergency Court of Appeals

The records of the Emergency Court of Appeals and the Temporary Emergency Court of Appeals are included with the Records of the U.S. Courts of Appeals in Record Group 276. The records of the Emergency Court of Appeals are held at the National Archives in Washington, D.C. The records of the Temporary Emergency Court of Appeals are available to researchers at the Washington National Records Center in Suitland, Maryland, pending their transfer to the National Archives.

## Foreign Intelligence Surveillance Court

The records of the Foreign Intelligence Surveillance Court remain classified and have not been accessioned by the National Archives and Records Administration. Upon accession, they will make up Record Group 477.

# Appendix E.  National Archives Locations

This appendix provides a list of National Archives research facilities throughout the United States. The list does not include regional records centers, affiliated archives, the National Personnel Records Center, or the presidential libraries. For a complete list of National Archives facilities, see http://www.archives.gov/locations/. When contacting a regional NARA facility by email, researchers are requested to include their name, mailing address, phone number, and email address in the body of the email.

## Anchorage

National Archives at Anchorage
654 West Third Avenue
Anchorage, Alaska  99501-2145
Telephone: 907-261-7820
Email: alaska.archives@nara.gov

## Atlanta

National Archives at Atlanta
5780 Jonesboro Road
Morrow, Georgia  30260
Telephone: 770-968-2100
Email: atlanta.archives@nara.gov

## Boston

National Archives at Boston
Frederick C. Murphy Federal Center
380 Trapelo Road
Waltham, Massachusetts 02452-6399
Telephone: 781-663-0130
Email: waltham.archives@nara.gov

## Chicago

National Archives at Chicago
7358 South Pulaski Road
Chicago, Illinois  60629-5898
Telephone: 773-948-9001
Email: chicago.archives@nara.gov

## College Park, MD

National Archives at College Park, MD
8601 Adelphi Road
College Park, Maryland  20740-6001
Telephone: 301-837-2000
Customer Service Center Telephone: 866-272-6272

## Denver

National Archives at Denver
Buildings 46 and 48
Denver Federal Center
West 6th Avenue and Kipling Street
Denver, Colorado  80225
Telephone: 303-407-5740
Email: denver.archives@nara.gov

## Fort Worth

National Archives at Fort Worth
501 West Felix Street
Building 1
Fort Worth, Texas  76115-3405
Telephone: 817-831-5620
Email: ftworth.archives@nara.gov

## Kansas City

National Archives at Kansas City
400 West Pershing Road
Kansas City, Missouri  64108
Telephone: 816-268-8000
Email: kansascity.archives@nara.gov

## New York City

National Archives at New York City
201 Varick Street
12th Floor
New York, New York  10014
Entrance on Houston Street, between Varick and Hudson.
Telephone: 866-840-1752 or 212-401-1620
Email: newyork.archives@nara.gov

## Philadelphia

National Archives at Philadelphia
900 Market Street
Philadelphia, Pennsylvania  19107-4292
Entrance on Chestnut Street, between 9th and 10th Streets.
Telephone: 215-606-0100
Email: philadelphia.archives@nara.gov

## Riverside

National Archives at Riverside
23123 Cajalco Road
Perris, California  92570-7298
Telephone: 951-965-2000
Email: riverside.archives@nara.gov

## San Francisco

National Archives at San Francisco
1000 Commodore Drive
San Bruno, California  94066-2350
Telephone: 650-238-3501
Email: sanbruno.archives@nara.gov

## Seattle

National Archives at Seattle
6125 Sand Point Way NE
Seattle, Washington  98115-7999
Telephone: 206-336-5115
Email: seattle.archives@nara.gov

## Washington, D.C.

National Archives Building in Washington
700 Pennsylvania Avenue NW
Washington, District of Columbia  20408-0001
Telephone: 202-357-5000
Customer Service Center Telephone: 866-325-7208

# Appendix F. Court Records Held Outside of the National Archives

Although the National Archives and Records Administration is the official custodian of the "permanently valuable records" of the United States government, some federal records are held outside of the National Archives system. Prior to the establishment of the National Archives in 1934, the federal government had no uniform system for the maintenance and preservation of official government records. Federal records were often stored in courthouses, post offices, customhouses, federal office buildings, and other locations throughout the United States. (In a few instances, federal courts still have their historic court records.) Between 1789 and the mid-twentieth century, many historic federal records were also transferred to nonfederal libraries and archival institutions.

Most of the historic records that had been accessioned by repositories outside of the federal government have since been transferred to the National Archives. However, a few collections of federal court records still exist outside of the NARA system. Below is a list of collections of historic court records that are held outside of the federal government.

The following list is based on keyword searches conducted in archival research databases. This list excludes microfilmed and photocopied records of originals held at the National Archives, trial and hearing transcripts, territorial court records, exhibits and case papers that were used by the litigants in court proceedings, copies of court records that were produced for use outside of the federal court system, and the official records of court officers, such as marshals and U.S. attorneys, that are held in personal research collections.

## U.S. District Court for the Western District of Arkansas

Western History Collections, University of Oklahoma, Norman, Okla.
Correspondence (1872–1903)

## U.S. Courts of California

## U.S. Circuit Courts for the Judicial Districts of California

University of California, Berkeley, Calif.
Minutes (1855–1911)
Minutes of court sessions held at Los Angeles (1857–1861)
Judgment record books (1855–1864)

Judgment record book in admiralty cases (1855–1861)
Equity degree register (1855–1861)
Judgment record in equity (1860–1863)
Judgment record at common law (1856–1862)
Rule book (1854–1911)

## U.S. District Court for the Northern District of California

University of California, Berkeley, Calif.
Private land claim cases, on loan from the court (ca. 1854–1861)
Notes from minute and decree books in private land cases (original records missing)
Records relating to land cases (1856–1905)
Case records from *Martin v. Crane* (1861)

## U.S. District Court for the Southern District of California

University of California, Berkeley, Calif.
Statement of expenditures (ca. 1850s)

## Courts of the District of Columbia

## Circuit Court of the District of Columbia (Alexandria sessions)

Library of Virginia, Richmond, Va.
Liber A (copies of indictments and case papers) (1801–1802)
Fee book (1807, 1846)
Volume of fines, penalties, and forfeitures (1801–1846)
Index to judgments (1801–1813)
Minute books (1801–1843)
Orders (1801–1827)
Docket of witnesses (1801–1817)
Record of actions in which the United States was the plaintiff (1836–1846)
Record of executions issued on judgment (1801–1807)
Rule book (1817–1819)
Trial dockets (1802–1822, with gaps)
Abstract of reports of aliens (1801–1830)

## District Court for the District of Potomac

Library of Virginia, Richmond, Va.
Minutes (1801–1802)

District Court for the District of Columbia (Alexandria sessions)

Library of Virginia, Richmond, Va.
Admiralty court orders (1803–1827)
Admiralty court records (1806–1830)
Bankruptcy proceedings (1802–1821)

Criminal Court of the District of Columbia (Alexandria sessions)

Library of Virginia, Richmond, Va.
Minute book (1838–1846)

Justices of the Peace of the District of Columbia (Alexandria sessions)

Library of Virginia, Richmond, Va.
Record of executions issued on judgment (1802–1807, 1816–1819)
Record of judgments (1824–1827)

Levy Court of the District of Columbia (Alexandria sessions)

Library of Virginia, Richmond, Va.
Minute book (1801–1827)

Orphans' Court of the District of Columbia (Alexandria sessions)

Library of Virginia, Richmond, Va.
Records (1801–1830, with gaps)
Minute book (1842–1847)

U.S. Circuit Court for the District of Southern Illinois

Abraham Lincoln Presidential Library, Springfield, Ill.
Clerk of court's account book (1860–1861)

U.S. District Court for the District of Kentucky

Filson Historical Society, Louisville, Ky.
Memorandum book (1799–1801)
Order book (1799–1801)
Reports of cases (1795, 1798–1800)
Legal opinions (1795–1806)

U.S. District Court for the District of Maryland

Library of Congress, Washington, D.C.
 Case record (1840)

U.S. Courts of New York

U.S. District Court for the Southern District of New York

New York Historical Society, New York City
 Minute book (1872)

U.S. Circuit Court for the Southern District of New York

New-York Historical Society, New York City
 New York State Legal Papers Collection (ca. 1779–1890)

U.S. District Court for the Western District of Oklahoma

Western History Collections, University of Oklahoma, Norman, Okla.
 Stenographers' notebooks (1893–1910)
 Books of statutes, cases, and rules of procedure (1873–1912)
 U.S. marshal's records (1890–1912)
 Clerk of court's records (1892–1921)
 Ledgers (1898–1935)
 Correspondence of the clerk of court and U.S. marshal (1894–1926)
 Photographs

U.S. Circuit Court for the Eastern District of Texas

Texas Tech University, Lubbock, Tex.
 Minutes (1879)
 Correspondence (1881–1911)

U.S. Courts of Virginia

U.S. Circuit Courts for the District of Virginia and the Eastern District of Virginia

Library of Virginia, Richmond, Va.
 Ended cases (1790–1861)
 Order books (1790–1831)
 Record books (1791–1834)
 Fee book (1835–1843)
 Rule books (1790–1845)
 Miscellaneous volumes

U.S. District Courts for the District of Virginia and the Eastern District of Virginia

Library of Virginia, Richmond, Va.
    Ended cases (1790–1861)
    Confiscations (dates not determined)
    Executions (1858–1861)
    Bankruptcies (1842–1845, 1861)
    Order books (1797–1874)
    Record books (1790–1873)
    Confiscations (1863–1869)
    Miscellaneous volumes and papers
    Miscellaneous indexes

U.S. District Court for the District of Wisconsin

Wisconsin Historical Society, Madison, Wisc.
    Judgment record book (1849–1859)

# Index

China, U.S. Court for. *See* U.S. Court for China

circuit courts. *See* U.S. circuit courts

circuit judicial conferences, 79

circuit judicial councils, 73, 78

civil jurisdiction: District of Columbia courts, 55–56; Judicial Panel on Multidistrict Litigation, 71; Justice Department, 139; U.S. attorney case files, 147–48; U.S. circuit courts, 26–28, 33; U.S. commissioners and, 23; U.S. Court of International Trade, 64; U.S. district courts, 7, 12–14, 20. *See also* rules and procedures

Civil Service Commission, U.S., 85

clerks of courts: administrative records, 9, 10–12, 19, 25, 32; Congress, reports to, 62, 93, 104; courts of appeals, 39–40; directories of, 143–44; Interior Department, correspondence with, 127; Justice Department, correspondence with, 136–37, 139, 140; marshals, correspondence with, 145; records, non-federal, 207–08; Supervising Architect, correspondence with, 152, 155; Supreme Court, 46–47, 50; Treasury Department, correspondence with, 113, 114, 116–17, 188, 119–20, 122. *See also* type of court

Commerce Court, 67–68, 139, 184

commissioners, 23–24, 25, 31–33, 142. *See also* magistrate judges

common law jurisdiction, 12–14, 26–28, 206

Confederate courts, 83–84

confiscations, 22–23, 121, 209

copyrights, 11, 13, 27, 36, 55, 110, 137

counterfeiting, 114, 119–20, 122–23, 124, 137

Court of Appeals for the Armed Forces. *See* U.S. Court of Appeals for the Armed Forces

Court of Appeals for Veterans Claims. *See* U.S. Court of Appeals for Veterans Claims

Court of Appeals in Cases of Capture, 83

Court of Claims: 60–62; Attorney General and, 131, 133, 134, 136, 140–41; correspondence regarding, 116, 117–18, 127; financial records, 128; guide to records, 185; published reports, 35; successor court, 63. *See also* U.S. Court of Federal Claims

Court of Customs and Patent Appeals. *See* U.S. Court of Customs and Patent Appeals

Court of Federal Claims. *See* U.S. Court of Federal Claims

Court of International Trade. *See* U.S. Court of International Trade

courthouses, 95, 96, 128, 139, 149–66, 178

courts of appeals. *See* U.S. courts of appeals

criminal jurisdiction: commissioners and, 23–24; in District of Columbia courts, 53, 54, 55–56, 193, 207; FBI and, 142–43; prosecutions, 110, 133, 135, 137, 139; rules, 35, 46, 133; Secret Service and, 122–23; sentencing guidelines, 79–81; U.S. attorneys and, 147–48; in U.S. circuit courts, 7, 28–29, 33; in U.S. courts of appeals, 37; in U.S. district courts, 7, 14–15, 22, 32, 83

Customs Court. *See* U.S. Customs Court

district courts. *See* U.S. district courts

District of Columbia courts: 53–57; administration of, 128; court of appeals, 38, 66; guide to records, 85, 185; justices of the peace, 112; prisoners in, 127; records, 206–07

election supervisors, 11, 14, 25–26, 27, 32–33

Emergency Court of Appeals, 68–70

equity jurisdiction: California court records, 206; in District of Columbia courts, 55; rules, 44; in U.S. circuit courts, 26–28, 31; in U.S. Court of International Trade, 64; in U.S. district courts, 12–14

Federal Bureau of Investigation, 142–43, 183

*Federal Cases*, 34–35, 56

Federal Judicial Center, 76–77, 177–80

*Federal Reporter*: 35; Commerce Court 68; Court of Claims reports, 62; District of Columbia courts, 57; Emergency Court of Appeals, 70; Foreign Intelligence Surveillance Court, 71; U.S. courts of appeals, 39, 41

*Federal Supplement*, 35, 57, 62, 65, 71, 72

Foreign Intelligence Surveillance Court, 70–71

fugitive slave cases, 13, 23, 24–25, 27, 31–32, 55

habeas corpus: in Confederate courts, 84, in District of Columbia courts, 55; in fugitive slave cases, 25, 32; in Supreme Court, 46; in U.S. circuit courts, 28, 29, 32; in U.S. district courts, 15–16, 24, 25

impeachment: 100–01; hearings, 97; House Judiciary Committee records, 93; judicial impeachments, 177; petitions regarding, 94; published proceedings, 102–03; records restrictions, 89; Senate journal, 90

Interior, Department of: 127–29; courthouse related correspondence, 153, 158, 161; House Judiciary Committee, correspondence with, 93; judiciary accounts, 113; records guide, 183; records transferred, 132, 137, 140; Supreme Court marshal, correspondence with, 48; Treasury Department, correspondence with, 124, 128

judges' papers, 169–70, 180

Judicial Conference of the United States, 71–72, 73–75, 77, 80, 179

Judicial Panel on Multidistrict Litigation, 35, 71–72

juries: expenses, 128, 137; findings, 9, 15; grand juries, 9, 11, 36, 50, 148; instructions, 10, 13, 27, 50; rooms, 161; selection and management, 9, 11, 15, 27, 28, 137

Justice, Department of: 131–48; courthouse related correspondence, 151, 153, 161; financial accounts, 124, 128; research guides, 183–84; Solicitor of the Treasury, correspondence with, 119, 121; Supreme Court Marshal, correspondence with, 48; Treasury Department, correspondence with, 113, 115–17

law cases, 12–14, 25, 26–28, 32, 55

magistrate judges, 23–24

maritime law. *See* admiralty jurisdiction

Marshal of the Supreme Court, 47–48

marshals, U.S.: 144–46; accounts, 93, 116, 128, 131, 137, 139, 142; appointment, 111–12, 127, 132, 140, 143; Attorney General and Justice Department, correspondence with, 133–34, 136–37; Commerce Court and, 68; court administration duties, 10, 11–12, 21–22; courthouse related correspondence, 155; fugitive slaves and, 25, 32; Interior Department, correspondence with, 127–28; Oklahoma, Western District records, 208; personal records, 170; records guides, 183; State Department, correspondence with, 109–10; Treasury Department, correspondence with, 114, 118, 119–20, 122

Merit Services Protection Board, 38

naturalization, 11, 18–20, 29–31, 55, 95, 96

nominations, judicial. *See* appointments

pardons, 28, 110, 112, 123, 141–42, 183

patents: appeals, 54, 55, 66–67; case files, 13, 27; congressional committees, 95–96; Court of Claims jurisdiction, 60; Justice Department files, 137–38; reports, 36

President of the United States: appointment authority, 7, 17, 54, 60, 67; appointments, administrative, 16, 64, 80, 118; appointments, records, 99–100, 111–12, 182; appropriations, judicial, 110; commissions, 111–12; correspondence, with Attorney General and Justice Department, 133–34, 136, 138; messages to Congress, 91, 103; papers, 171–72; pardons, 28, 112, 141–42. *See also* appointments, judicial

prize cases: 20–22; executive branch correspondence, 110, 117, 120, 128; marshals' records, 146; pre-federal, 83; records guide, 185; reports, 34

Reporters, Supreme Court, 48–50

rules and procedures: Administrative Office of the U.S. Courts, 75–76; Attorney General, 133; circuit judicial councils, 78; courts of special jurisdiction, 59, 69, 71–72; Judicial Conference, 73; Supreme Court, 44, 46, 51; U.S. circuit courts, 9–11; U.S. courts of appeals, 39, 41–42; U.S. district courts, 9–11, 13–14, 20–21, 35; Virginia federal court records, 208

Secret Service, U.S., 122–23, 184

Sentencing Commission, U.S., 79–81, 179

Solicitor General of the United States, 132, 135, 138

Solicitor of the Court of Claims, 133, 134

Solicitor of the Treasury, 115, 116, 118–22, 123, 134, 157

State, Department of, 84, 109–12, 132, 141, 182

Supervising Architect, Office of the, 149–50, 151–56, 161, 165

Supreme Court of the United States: 43–51; accounts, 116, 128; Administrative Office of the U.S. Courts and, 75; appointments, 138, 140; bankruptcy decisions, 35; building, 158; circuit allotments, 144; documentary histories, 104–05; Justice Department case files, 134, 135, 139; mandates, 34, 40; nontextual records, 43; records guides, 183–85; reporters' papers, 170–71; Solicitor of the Treasury and, 120; sound recordings, 43

**About the Federal Judicial Center**

The Federal Judicial Center is the research and education agency of the federal judicial system. It was established by Congress in 1967 (28 U.S.C. §§ 620–629), on the recommendation of the Judicial Conference of the United States.

By statute, the Chief Justice of the United States chairs the Center's Board, which also includes the director of the Administrative Office of the U.S. Courts and seven judges elected by the Judicial Conference.

The organization of the Center reflects its primary statutory mandates. The Education Division plans and produces education and training programs for judges and court staff, including satellite broadcasts, video programs, publications, curriculum packages for in-court training, and Web-based programs and resources. The Research Division examines and evaluates current and alternative federal court practices and policies. This research assists Judicial Conference committees, who request most Center research, in developing policy recommendations. The Center's research also contributes substantially to its educational programs. The two divisions work closely with two units of the Director's Office—the Systems Innovations & Development Office and Communications Policy & Design Office—in using print, broadcast, and online media to deliver education and training and to disseminate the results of Center research. The Federal Judicial History Office helps courts and others study and preserve federal judicial history. The International Judicial Relations Office provides information to judicial and legal officials from foreign countries and assesses how to inform federal judicial personnel of developments in international law and other court systems that may affect their work.

www.ingramcontent.com/pod-product-compliance
Lightning Source LLC
Chambersburg PA
CBHW080245290526
45790CB00005B/1705